D0721164

Far More Precious than Jewels

Gender and the Biblical Tradition

Far More Precious than Jewels

Perspectives on Biblical Women

Katheryn Pfisterer Darr

Westminster/John Knox Press
Louisville, Kentucky

Unless otherwise noted, scripture quotations are from *Tanakh,* copyright 1985 by The Jewish Publication Society, and are used by permission.

Scripture quotations marked RSV are from the Revised Standard Version of the Bible, copyrighted 1946, 1952, © 1971, 1973 by the Division of Christian Education of the National Council of the Churches of Christ in the U.S.A., and are used by permission.

Frontispiece artwork is copyright © 1991 by Pem Pfisterer Clark, and is used by permission.

Book design by Ken Taylor

First edition

Published by Westminster/John Knox Press
Louisville, Kentucky

PRINTED IN THE UNITED STATES OF AMERICA
9   8   7   6   5   4   3   2

Library of Congress Cataloging-in-Publication Data

Darr, Katheryn Pfisterer, 1952–
  Far more precious than jewels : perspectives on biblical women / Katheryn Pfisterer Darr. — 1st ed.
        p.   cm. — (Gender and the biblical tradition)
  Includes bibliographical references and index.
  ISBN 0-664-25107-2

  1. Women in the Bible   2. Bible.   O.T.—Biography.   3. Bible and feminism.   I. Title.   II. Series.
BS575.D33   1991
220.9′2—dc20   91-4516

Dedication

For my sister,
Pem Pfisterer Clark,
a very accomplished woman;
and for our beloved parents,
Fred R. and Ann Rader Pfisterer,
who raised two daughters without ever suggesting
that gender limited possibilities.

Contents

Preface

Every year, Boston University's Anna Howard Shaw Research and Reference Center sponsors a Women's Study Series—an opportunity for women from local churches to gather with women students, administrators, and faculty from Boston University School of Theology for study and fellowship. When Margaret Wiborg, director of the Shaw Center, invited me to present a paper during the 1986 Series, I was completing a straightforward article on the book of Ruth for a new reference work. Hoping that my research for that project might serve double duty, I considered presenting a talk on Ruth. But how, I wondered, could I make a lecture on that topic interesting for women who, I knew, had heard her story many times before? At length, I decided to present the biblical narrative but to supplement it with insights from three quite diverse constituencies: modern critical biblical specialists, rabbinical interpreters, and feminist scholars. Responses to that lecture, an early version of chapter two in this book, were quite positive. In particular, women expressed interest in the rabbinical materials—an entirely new resource for many of them—and surprise at the diversity of opinions articulated by contemporary female interpreters of Scripture.

In October, 1988, I was privileged to deliver the third annual Edward L. Beavin Memorial Lectures at my alma mater, Kentucky Wesleyan College, in Owensboro, Kentucky. These lectures were established in honor of Dr. Beavin (may his memory long remain), an outstanding teacher of the Hebrew Bible whose impact on many students, myself included, simply can never be calculated. In addition to a revised version of the Ruth lecture, I also wrote for that occasion a lecture on Hagar (an early version of chapter four) and a sermon about Sarah (on which chapter three is based). The Esther lecture, revised and included here in chapter five, was added when I was invited to lead a continuing education event for the clergy of the Presbytery of the Pines at LeGray State Park, Arkansas, in October, 1989.

I am grateful to my husband, Dr. John A. Darr, Assistant Professor of New Testament at Boston College, and to my colleagues, Drs. Simon B. Parker, J. Paul Sampley, and Carter Lindberg, for reading the manuscript with great care and offering many helpful comments and suggestions. I also thank my student, Rabbi Lawrence Arthur Forman, and especially George I. Dees, for critiquing the section on Jewish interpretation of scripture and teaching me a great deal in the process. Another student, Eileen Noyes-Verchereau, checked all references, saving me from a number of errors. Finally, a special word of appreciation goes to Drs. John Combs and C. Bob Darrell, professors of English at Kentucky Wesleyan College, who sit on my shoulders whenever I write.

When the author of Proverbs 31:10–31 wrote that an accomplished woman is "far more precious than jewels," he was, I think, stating that such a woman is not only invaluable, but also rare. I have been blessed, however, to know many accomplished women—family members, friends, colleagues, and students. As I complete this manuscript, I am thinking of them.

K. P. D.

1

More than Historical Criticism: Critical, Rabbinical, and Feminist Perspectives on Biblical Interpretation

Introduction

The title of this book, *Far More Precious than Jewels,* is a quotation from Proverbs 31:10 (RSV), the initial verse of an acrostic poem in praise of the accomplished woman.[1] This entertaining—and exhausting—poem describes the endless activities of an ancient Israelite superwoman who joyfully devotes all her time and energy to the smooth, efficient management of her household, thereby freeing her husband to attend to the public affairs of a "man's world."

It is fair to say that different interpreters have interpreted this text differently. For the early rabbis, the poem raised some interesting questions. Who was this King

Lemuel referred to at the beginning of the chapter (31:1), and why did his mother admonish him? What was the true identity of the woman extolled in verses 10–31? How could the text claim that she plants her own vineyard (v. 16) when, one Jewish commentator insisted, everyone knows that physical labor is unbecoming to a woman?[2] What made her husband so "prominent in the gates" (v. 23)?

The text raises questions for modern critical biblical scholars, too, although theirs are likely to be of quite a different sort. When and why was the poem composed, they ask, and by whom? What was its original setting in Israelite society? Can it shed light on the actual lives of women in biblical times?

Modern feminist interpreters of scripture, many of whom are trained in the methods of critical biblical scholarship, are interested in historical, social, and literary questions, as well. But they also ask whether this woman, for all her strength, initiative, and skill, is an appropriate role model for contemporary women. Should females be taught that only their endless efforts on behalf of others are praiseworthy? Is the tightly structured acrostic form itself an attempt to keep this accomplished woman firmly under (male) control?[3]

Our interpretations of literature, including biblical literature, are determined in large measure by the questions we bring to the text. And our questions are shaped, to no small extent, by who we are—very young or seasoned by experience, male or female, Jewish or Christian, at the top of a modern society's hierarchies, or poor members of an oppressed group. A third world liberation theologian, for example, probably approaches the Bible with presuppositions and questions that differ from those of an American specialist trained at a research university. Moreover, we are, inevitably, products of our time. The early rabbis did not interpret texts as would a 1990s woman with a Ph.D. in biblical studies. It is hardly surprising, therefore, that one can find an astonishing variety of perspectives on virtually every biblical passage. After all, the Hebrew scriptures (traditionally called the "Old Testament" by Christians) have been widely studied throughout the world by both Jews and Christians for more than two millennia.

Most people have had little opportunity to explore this fascinating history of interpretation. We scrutinize a biblical text, assisted perhaps by a commentary from the library at our church or temple. We may study a story in Sunday school. Perhaps we have seen movies about biblical characters. We nevertheless are unaware of the many insights and perspectives that can take us beyond our own limited focus, making our encounter with a character or tradition especially memorable. This book gives you, the reader, an opportunity to listen to a rich mix of voices, and to learn new ways of understanding the stories of four biblical women—Ruth, Sarah, Hagar, and Esther.[4]

Some of these voices may be foreign to you. Many Christians know virtually nothing about the vast bodies of interpretive literature produced by Jews during the centuries following the completion of their Bible. Some Christian and Jewish readers may never have been exposed to the methods of critical biblical scholarship or to feminist interpretations of scripture. This first chapter, therefore, is a brief introduction to these different approaches: critical, rabbinical, and feminist. We shall begin with the modern critical approach—scholarship that, despite the negative connotations of the word "critical," has shed extraordinary light on ancient Israel's culture, history, religion, society, and literary artistry.

Modern Critical Approaches to the Hebrew Bible

For many people, the idea of using scholarly methods of inquiry to analyze the Bible seems strange, even threatening. They are accustomed to reading scripture for the spiritual light it can shed on their lives rather than for information about the distant past. Biblical scholars do not deny scripture's religious significance for today. On the contrary, many of these scholars are members of churches or synagogues; when a scriptural passage is read on Sunday morning, or on the Jewish Sabbath, they listen for the word of God. They presuppose, however, that human beings also had a hand in the creation of the Bible, and that its religious truths are expressions of a particular people, living in specific times and places.

Modern critical biblical scholarship seeks to recover information about the world of ancient Israel—its culture, history, religion, society, and literature—through disciplined application of the same methods used in the study of secular literature. This goal need not be pursued in the service of church or synagogue, although both institutions may benefit from it. For biblical scholars teaching in colleges and research universities, as well as in most seminaries, learning about ancient Israel is an intrinsically valuable task that should be pursued, even if traditional views of the Bible are challenged in the process.[5]

The Rise of Historical-Critical Biblical Scholarship

Critical approaches to the Bible are, historically, a relatively recent phenomenon. For centuries, biblical study and interpretation were the responsibility of rabbis and church leaders, and woe to those who challenged their views or questioned the Bible's veracity. Scripture was accorded the highest authority, not only for theological studies, but also in matters of science and history, for it was believed to be the incontestable word of the omniscient God.

During the Renaissance of the fourteenth through sixteenth centuries, however, this venerable structure of traditional biblical interpretation began to crack. A fresh interest in antiquity prompted the collection of biblical manuscripts. The invention of the printing press made it possible to reproduce these texts in large numbers; and suddenly, the Bible was much more accessible to both clergy and laity. Christian scholars eagerly learned the biblical languages—Hebrew and Greek—required for serious study of these manuscripts.[6] Despite severe censure from the Church, the Renaissance humanists began to study the Bible using the identical analytical methods applied to ancient Greek and Roman literature.

In the sixteenth century, the Protestant Reformation made possible the fresh examination of a Bible not bound by centuries-old ecclesiastical interpretations. The Reformers in no way wished to undercut biblical authority. On the contrary, Luther gave "primacy to Scripture in all questions that are referred to the church fathers. This means that [Scripture] itself by itself is the most unequivocal, the most accessible, the most comprehensible authority, itself its own interpreter, attesting, judging, and illuminating all things. . . . "[7] By their emphasis on the literal, historical meaning of biblical texts, however, the Reformers helped prepare the way for historical-critical investigation.

A more direct challenge to long-standing ideas about biblical authority was the growth of knowledge. In the seventeenth century, philosophy, science, and history—now independent fields, largely detached from theological constraints—challenged old ways of thinking and garnered evidence that contradicted biblical views about creation, cosmology, and so on. In short, both biblical interpretation and traditional views of biblical authority were in flux, challenged by the new perspectives, questions, and ideas that accompany changing times. By the end of the eighteenth-century Enlightenment, historical-critical interpretation of the Bible was well under way, first in German universities and then throughout the Western world.

The Tools of Historical-Critical Biblical Scholarship

For all that the Bible says, it maintains a discreet silence concerning many issues of crucial interest to historical critics. In the Hebrew Bible, all too many writings are anonymous and undated.[8] We are not told, for example, who wrote the Pentateuch or when it was composed.[9] Tradition attributes it to Moses, but the Bible itself makes no such claim. As early as the twelfth century, the great rabbi Ibn Ezra questioned whether Moses could have written at least some portions of the written Torah.[10] His cautious observations were followed some five centuries later by the plainspoken arguments of Benedict de Spinoza. Insisting that the Bible, like any other book, should be subjected to autonomous human reason, Spinoza listed his reasons for rejecting Mosaic authorship of the entire Pentateuch, including the following:

> We must also remark that the history relates not only the manner of Moses' death and burial, and the thirty days' mourning of the Hebrews, but further compares him with all the prophets who came after him, and states that he surpassed them all. "There was never a prophet in Israel like unto Moses, whom the Lord knew face to face," declares Scripture. Such testimony cannot have been given by Moses himself, nor by any who immediately succeeded him, but it must come from someone who lived centuries afterwards.[11]

In addition to their awareness of such anachronisms, source critics of the seventeenth, eighteenth, and nineteenth centuries cited differences in vocabulary for the same persons and places,[12] contradictions,[13] and variations in literary style and theological perspective as evidence that the Pentateuch actually contained four literary sources: the Yahwistic, or "J" source (so called for its preference for the personal divine name,

YHWH);[14] the Elohistic source (in which Elohim, "God," is the favored designation for Israel's deity); and the Priestly materials, characterized by their concern for religious purity and ritual. The "D" source, so called because it appears almost exclusively in the book of Deuteronomy, was widely held to be the law scroll discovered in Jerusalem in 621 B.C.E.[15] and instrumental in the religious reforms of the Judean king Josiah (see 2 Kings 22:8–20). Scholars were uncertain in what order the three remaining sources were composed, however, until a German scholar named Julius Wellhausen (1844–1918), the son of a Protestant pastor, built a convincing argument that the Priestly writers' contributions were the latest of the four sources.[16] Today, the majority of biblical scholars agree that the Yahwistic source dates from about 950 B.C.E., the Elohistic from around 850 B.C.E., and the Priestly work between 500 and 450 B.C.E.[17] Many specialists also believe that after the destruction of Northern Israel by the Assyrians in 721 B.C.E., the Yahwistic and Elohistic sources were combined to form a single narrative. This source, sometimes called the "Old Epic narrative," was adopted by the Priestly editors, who nevertheless transformed it by reworking and supplementing the material.[18]

A sample biblical text, submitted to source-critical analysis, illustrates some of the evidence for pentateuchal sources. The following passage from Exodus describes one of the plagues that afflicted Egypt after Pharaoh refused Moses' demand to release his Hebrew slaves. In what follows, verses attributed to the Old Epic narrative are printed in italics, while verses contributed by "P" appear in regular type.

> [14]*And the LORD said to Moses, "Pharaoh is stubborn; he refuses to let the people go. *[15]*Go to Pharaoh in the morning, as he is coming out to the water, and station yourself before him at the edge of the Nile, taking with you the rod that turned into a snake. *[16]*And say to him, "The LORD, the God*

of the Hebrews, sent me to you to say, 'Let My people go that they may worship Me in the wilderness.' But you have paid no heed until now. [17]*Thus says the* LORD, *"By this you shall know that I am the* LORD." *See, I shall strike the water in the Nile with the rod that is in my hand, and it will be turned into blood;* [18]*and the fish in the Nile will die. The Nile will stink so that the Egyptians will find it impossible to drink the water of the Nile.*

[19]And the LORD said to Moses, "Say to Aaron: Take your rod and hold out your arm over the waters of Egypt—its rivers, its canals, its ponds, all its bodies of water—that they may turn to blood; there shall be blood throughout the land of Egypt, even in vessels of wood and stone." [20]Moses and Aaron did just as the LORD had commanded: *he lifted up the rod and struck the water in the Nile* in the sight of Pharaoh and his courtiers, *and all the water in the Nile was turned into blood* [21]*and the fish in the Nile died. The Nile stank so that the Egyptians could not drink water from the Nile;* and there was blood throughout the land of Egypt. [22]But when the Egyptian magicians did the same with their spells, Pharaoh's heart stiffened and he did not heed them—as the LORD had spoken. [23]*Pharaoh turned and went into his palace, paying no regard even to this.* [24]*And all Egyptians had to dig round about the Nile for drinking water, because they could not drink the water of the Nile*[19] (Exod. 7:14–24).

On first reading, this passage appears to be a unified account of God's order to Moses, its execution, and Pharaoh's response. Look more carefully, however, and you will discover that while God speaks only to Moses in the Old Epic narrative, the Priestly writers are careful to include Aaron in the story as well. In fact, the authors of "P" make Aaron the principal actor. In verse 17 (Old Epic), Moses was himself instructed to strike the Nile with his staff; but in verse 19 ("P"), Moses simply conveys to Aaron God's order that he, Aaron, hold his staff over the waters of Egypt.[20] The Priestly writers' desire to emphasize Aaron's role in events is understandable, of course, since Aaron was Israel's first high priest. But there are other differences between these sources as well. According to the older rendition, only the Nile River was changed into blood. After it was polluted, the Egyptians were forced to dig wells for their water (v. 24). According to the Priestly editors, however, all of the water in Egypt —even that stored in jars—turned into blood (v. 19). The tendency to heighten the miraculous nature of divine acts is characteristic of "P." In this context, however, it creates a problem: Where, one wonders, did the Egyptian magicians obtain water to perform the identical spell (v. 22) if, as verse 19 states would be the case, every drop of water in Egypt had already been turned into blood?

Source-critical analysis is not, of course, limited to the Pentateuch. It may profitably be applied to any composite literary work. Nevertheless, the identification of pentateuchal sources and their dates was a tremendous boon to early critical biblical scholarship. Suddenly, the Pentateuch was recognized as an invaluable source of information not only for the ancient times and events it detailed, but also for those subsequent periods in Israel's history when its sources were composed, combined, and edited.

Identifying the approximate date when a source was written down, however, does not necessarily shed much light upon the age of various materials (stories, poems, and so forth) within that source. In the wake of Wellhausen's work, scholars—most notably Hermann Gunkel —became increasingly aware that many materials in the Pentateuch circulated independently, in oral form, for decades and even centuries prior to their inclusion in the written sources. Gunkel, called the father of form criticism, and his followers identified ancient Israel's many types of oral literature—narratives, proverbs, hymns, laments, love songs, and so on—and sought to discern their beginnings, endings, and internal structures (in short, their forms) as well as to identify their original settings and functions within Israelite society. Consider, for example, our poem about the accomplished woman (Prov. 31:10–31). In English translation, the poem's form is impossible to discern. Read in Hebrew, however, it is hard to miss, for the acrostic pattern is striking. Determining the boundaries of an acrostic is not difficult, because it is easy to tell where the poem begins and ends.[21] It is clear, as well, that the acrostic form is, at the very least, a mnemonic device, an aid to memory. If you know that the first word of the first verse begins with an *aleph*, the first word of the second verse with a *bet*, and so on through the letters of the Hebrew alphabet, you're unlikely to mix up the lines or forget them altogether.

Form critics ask additional questions, however, that are more difficult to answer. What, for example, was this particular poem's original setting in the life of ancient Israel? Does its didactic intent suggest that it is part of Israel's wisdom literature, the product of its sages? What was its purpose? Was it intended to provide young women with a role model, or to guide young men in their choice of a wife? Where was it learned and recited—at home, as later Jewish practice suggests?[22] Or was it taught in a school setting? Answers to these questions are discovered, in part, by examining other biblical texts having the same form, or genre, as the pericope being analyzed.[23] With the unearthing of ancient texts composed by Israel's neighbors, moreover, scholars have discovered similarities between biblical literature and the larger literary world of the ancient Near East and have benefited enormously from access to a much larger body of comparative literature.[24]

Source criticism, form criticism, and the comparative study of other ancient Near Eastern texts are not the only resources available to historical critics. Using a tradition-history approach, scholars trace the dynamic process by which biblical traditions about particular themes (e.g., creation, exodus, murmuring in the wilderness) were formed and passed down from one generation to the next. In the course of transmission, such traditions rarely remained static; and the tradition-history approach helps scholars identify those factors—social, political, and economic, as well as religious—that caused the modification of traditions over the centuries.

Finally, redaction criticism focuses the critic's attention upon the motivations of biblical editors who collected, arranged, modified and supplemented traditional materials. Read, for example, 2 Kings 17:1–18, the account of Northern Israel's destruction by the Assyrians in 721 B.C.E. The anonymous editors of this material begin with a straightforward, historical account of King Hoshea's rebellion and the Assyrians' crushing reprisal. In vs. 7–18, however, the editors shift from history to their own theology, explaining Israel's demise as the end result of its long-lived failure to hear and obey God's demand for absolute fidelity. Although the editors do not reveal their names, locations, or date of composition, these verses disclose their theological perspective in a nutshell.

To this list of methodological aids one must, of course, add the discovery of material remains by archaeologists. Although archaeology has often been unable to verify biblical claims about history, it has contributed substantially to our understanding of life in ancient Israel.[25]

These, then, are some of the principal methods and resources used by practitioners of the historical-critical method to reconstruct the world of ancient Israel. Historical criticism has made possible the recovery of much of Israel's history, and the discovery, at least in part, of the ways in which the biblical literature was produced, preserved, and shaped into its final, or canonical, form. It has facilitated the identification of Israel's literary genres and recovered some of their original settings. The historical-critical method is well suited to the tasks it was designed to accomplish, and it has been remarkably successful. However, in recent decades, biblical scholars have recognized that many of their questions cannot be answered through historical-critical analysis. As a result, other methods have entered the sphere of biblical studies. Contemporary biblical scholarship requires more than the historical-critical method.

The Social Science and New Literary Approaches to the Hebrew Bible

The limitations of historical-critical methods of analysis have encouraged specialists to explore alternative approaches to the text. Two broad trends may be discerned in this development. On the one hand, scholars whose interests remain primarily historical have looked to the social sciences—sociology and anthropology—for more sophisticated methods of recovering ancient Israel's social structures. On the other hand, literary critics have focused upon the integrity and artistry of biblical texts in their final, canonical forms.[26]

The Social Sciences and the Bible

Social science methods, like the historical-critical method, seek to recover information about the world of ancient Israel. Their principal focus, therefore, is not the text itself, but rather the reality lying behind it. While historical criticism has traditionally been preoccupied with questions of religious and political history, a social science approach seeks to illumine the structures and workings of ancient Israelite society.[27] Norman Gottwald has summarized the social sciences agenda:

> Within the social science paradigm there is broad concurrence that the biblical writings were rooted in interacting groups of people organized in social structures that controlled the chief aspects of public life, such as family, economy, government, law, war, ritual, and religious belief. . . . The guiding question for social science approaches becomes, "What social structures and

social processes are explicit or implicit in the biblical literature, in the scattered socioeconomic data it contains, in the overtly political history it recounts, and in the religious beliefs and practices it attests?"[28]

The Bible preserves valuable information about ancient Israel's social structures, of course, but its data are far from complete. After all, the biblical authors and editors worked for specific, usually religious purposes; it was not their intention to provide future readers with sociological blueprints of the day-to-day operations of biblical Israel's institutions. Comparative literature from other ancient Near Eastern countries can shed some additional light but still cannot fill all of the gaps in our knowledge of Israelite society. Biblical social scientists must, therefore, make use of sociological and anthropological models based upon data gleaned from other societies, extinct and extant, that were and are in some aspects potentially similar to ancient Israelite society. "Granted that important social data are lacking for ancient Israel," says Gottwald, "we can form testable models for conceiving the society that are necessary to interpreting the knowledge that we do have and suggestive of additional research needed to refine or revise our tentative mappings of biblical society."[29]

Consider, for example, ancient Israelite prophecy. Historical-critical analysis has sought to learn as much as possible about the individual prophets, despite the Bible's paucity of biographical information. Greatest emphasis has been placed, however, upon the prophetic word.[30] What historical situation does an oracle address? What are the forms of prophetic oracles? Are those forms endemic to prophecy, or did the prophets borrow them from other settings—judicial, liturgical, or sapiential—in the community? What theological perspectives do particular prophetic sayings, or oracles, presuppose and articulate? Scholarship's preoccupation with the prophetic word is understandable, of course. But the presence in

ancient Israel of prophetic intermediaries—that is, persons who serve as conduits between the divine and human spheres—raises other sorts of issues as well. Social
scientists wonder, for example, how Israelite society influenced its prophets: What role did society play in their
selection and validation? What constraints did it place
upon prophetic activity? How, in turn, did the prophets
respond to feedback from their audiences? The Bible
provides, at best, partial answers to these questions. By
examining comparative data, however, and by employing
models developed through analysis of other societies in
which intermediation occurs, social scientists are able to
increase our understanding of prophecy's complex,
changing roles in ancient Israel.[31]

Of course, practitioners of this approach must exercise
caution, lest they be misled by superficial similarities between societies. Each human community is, after all, ultimately unique. Nevertheless, the social science approach
holds great promise for future biblical studies. Viewing
the Bible as "a social document that reflects the history
of changing social structures, functions, and roles in ancient Israel over a thousand years or so,"[32] social scientists help reconstruct Israel's complex, interconnected,
and dynamic society, the crucible in which Hebrew scripture was created.

New Literary Approaches to the Bible

While both historical criticism and social science approaches to the Hebrew Bible use biblical texts essentially
as a means to an end—the recovery of ancient Israel's
world—literary critics regard these works as ends in
themselves. What the text as it now appears is and does is
intrinsically valuable. Literature creates a unique, fictive
world, and that world should be analyzed on its own literary terms before the subject of its possible relation to the
real world is broached.[33] Speaking about those who
search for evidence of a text's historical assemblage and

fragment the text in the process, Robert Alter writes, "I have no quarrel with the courage of conjecture of those engaged in what Sir Edmund Leach has shrewdly called 'unscrambling the omelette,' but the essential point for the validity of the literary perspective is that we have in the Bible, with far fewer exceptions than the historical critics would allow, a very well-made omelette indeed." Alter urges us to enjoy tasting the omelette as omelette, rather than spending all our time trying to unscramble its originally discrete ingredients.[34]

Literary approaches to the Bible are as numerous and complex as the vast body of modern literary theory upon which they draw; and we cannot begin to survey even the most recent major developments and models.[35] For our purposes, it suffices to say that once the critic's attention shifts from the prehistory of a text to the text itself, it becomes possible, utilizing the tools of modern literary criticism, to examine its plot and character development, the narrator's point of view, rhetorical strategies, use of figurative language, and so on. Literary criticism cannot, and does not, seek to recover the hard data—the "stones and bones"—of history. It can, however, disclose the artistry of biblical narrative, increasing our knowledge of ancient Israel's literary conventions and enhancing our appreciation for the biblical authors' legacy.[36]

Jewish Interpretation of Scripture

As we have seen, modern biblical scholars employ critical methods to learn as much as possible about the history, religion, society, and literature of ancient Israel. They presuppose that the Bible, like any other literature, can be the object of critical scrutiny; and they regard the knowledge derived from such inquiry as in-

trinsically valuable. Their analyses need not be constrained by the traditional interpretations of church or
synagogue. Modern historical critics do not, for example,
resist evidence that the Pentateuch developed over a
lengthy period of Israel's history and through the combi-
nation of originally discrete literary sources. Quite the
contrary, such evidence enhances the critic's appreciation of these texts, because the Pentateuch then becomes
a valuable source of information not only for the ancient
times about which it speaks, but also for those periods
when its sources were composed, combined, and edited.

Traditional Jewish interpretation of scripture has not
proceeded from a historical-critical perspective, however.
While critical approaches to the Bible have been developed only during the past two and a half centuries or so,
the Jewish people have revered and scrutinized their biblical literature for two and a half millennia, confident that
it reveals who and what God wants Israel to be. Indeed,
scripture and its interpretation have played a major role
in shaping and maintaining Jewish self-identity, in sustaining Jewish communities and uniting them, despite
their diverse settings and situations, across the centuries.

Torah: Written and Oral

According to Jewish tradition, scripture comes from
God. Of greatest authority, owing to its legal content and
Mosaic origin, is Torah ("teaching" or "law").[37] While the
Israelites were encamped at Mt. Sinai, God gave to them,
through Moses, all of the instructions necessary for faithful living. The Written Torah is, of course, what modern
scholars call the Pentateuch, but the rabbis claimed that
God's gift to Israel at Sinai did not consist of Written
Torah alone. The Lord also gave Moses the Oral Torah—
a vast body of additional teachings that were, they insisted, equal in authority to the Written Law. Indeed,

Oral Torah was the indispensible corrollary and interpreter of Written Law. The inscribed Torah alone did not
speak to every situation in which questions of right conduct arose. Moreover, when situations were addressed,
information was often incomplete. Work on the Sabbath
was prohibited, for example (Exod. 20:8–11; Deut. 5:12–
15), but what exactly constituted work? Apparent incon-
sistencies existed,[38] and the wording was lamentably obscure at points.[39] "The statutes of the Written Law could
not have been fulfilled literally even in the generation in
which they were given," writes Moshe David Herr. "Even
those statutes of the Torah that appear to be clearly for-
mulated and detailed contain more that is obscure and
requires explanation than what is manifest and understandable."[40] Oral Torah provided the needed explanations.

Now this Oral Torah was, the rabbis affirmed, taught
by the leaders of one generation to those of the next,
throughout the centuries, down to their own day. The
great twelfth-century Torah scholar and philosopher Maimonides agreed: "All the laws of the Torah—that is, the
Oral Torah—have been received and handed down from
teacher to pupil (through the ages) up to Ezra (and
thence) up to Moses our teacher."[41] So long as the Jews
were living in their homeland, the rabbis claimed, this
handing-on process continued without interruption.
With the exile of many Jews to Babylon, however, there
was a danger that Oral Torah would be forgotten; and
this threat continued during the uncertain and often dangerous centuries of the post-exilic period.[42] For this reason, therefore, Oral Torah was finally committed to
writing about 200 C.E. in the form of Mishnah (from the
verb *shana,* "to repeat," "to learn by repetition").[43] To be
sure, the Mishnah was not a complete articulation of the
Oral Torah. It was, in fact, more like a collection of notes
intended to jog the memory, thereby eliciting fuller interpretations. In time, however, these fuller interpretations
(the *Gemara,* or "completion") also were committed to

writing and were combined with the Mishnah to create the Talmuds—the Palestinian Talmud about 370 C.E. and the Babylonian Talmud about 500 C.E.

Contemporary historians, including some Jewish scholars, have questioned this traditional reconstruction of Oral Torah's origins and transmission history. They point to literary evidence that among the diverse Jewish groups of the early Common Era, there was considerable disagreement about what constituted correct religious practice.[44] Eventually, scholars argue, one of these groups, the Pharisees, made the astonishing claim that their practices, judgments and scriptural interpretations were Oral Torah—revealed to Moses at Sinai, but taught orally by the leaders of each generation to their students. Their claim placed all of the exegetical and traditional practices of the Pharisees beneath the umbrella of Mosaic authority.[45] Historical critics believe, however, that the Pharisees' "Oral Torah" was actually a diverse body of material originating in different places and at various times in Jewish history. Its acceptance as the Sinai-given, perfectly transmitted complement to Written Law represented the triumph of Pharisaic interpretation and practice over the views and customs of competing groups.[46]

Moreover, the Pharisees' success in establishing the Mosaic authority of Oral Torah was, scholars claim, a key element in Judaism's survival, because the written Torah—inscribed and therefore immutable—could not by itself address the ever changing circumstances and new questions of subsequent generations. Oral Torah gave to its counterpart a flexibility that Written Torah could never have had in isolation. As Abraham Cohen has observed, "The Torah could never grow antiquated so long as it was capable of reinterpretation to comply with new contingencies."[47]

Were the Pharisees and their successors, the rabbis living after the destruction of the Jerusalem temple in 70 C.E., self-conscious innovators, or did they actually believe that the practices and interpretations they had learned from their teachers originated at Sinai? We can never answer this question with absolute certainty, for we cannot know everything that was in their minds. Their literature, however, supports the traditional Jewish view that these religious leaders did not define themselves as innovators. Repeatedly, they based their views upon the authority of their predecessors' interpretations, speaking in their names and placing greatest stock in the oldest opinions. Moreover, they were intent on preserving the entire interpretive tradition. Two opinions might conflict, but the rabbis did not discard one or the other for that reason. Rather, they sought to reconcile opposing views, or simply allowed them to coexist.

Halakhah and Aggadah

The Oral Torah embraced an enormous variety of literary types which could, nevertheless, be grouped beneath two broad rubrics: *Halakhah* and *Aggadah*. The former (from the root *hlk* meaning, "to walk, go," but also "to behave, conduct oneself") referred to rabbinic explications of Judaism's obligatory religious observances, legal requirements, and judicial decisions. They were, in other words, the way in which Israel was "to walk." In contrast, Aggadah ("proclamation," "lesson," from the root *ngd* meaning, "to declare," "to proclaim") consisted of rabbinic reflections on nonlegal biblical texts, practices, and customs for didactical and homiletical (preaching) purposes. Halakhah's authority exceeded that of Aggadah (pl. Aggadoth). When the rabbis interpreted legal texts and customs, or ruled on legal practices, their halakhic judgments were binding. When a rabbi proclaimed Aggadah, however, his audience was not required to agree with his views.

Because of its obligatory nature, scholars often regard Halakhah as the more important of the two bodies of

material. It is true, of course, that Torah observance was
Judaism's overriding responsibility and concern, for God
expressly commanded that Israel keep Torah, *do* Torah.
But Aggadah played a crucial role as well; and the same
rabbis were involved in both halakhic and aggadic teaching. The two were simply different ways of thinking about
texts. Halakhah required meticulous study of Torah according to established methods of interpretation, or hermeneutics. It entailed in-depth exploration of traditional
interpretations, and the careful weighing of competing
arguments. Aggadah, by contrast, required the imagination of a mind disciplined in Torah, but then set free.
Included in the Aggadah were the legends, folklore,
prayers, fables, and pleasantries gleaned from their
teachers and stored in the rabbis' memories.[48] In the
academies, teachers and their students carried out the
complex and painstaking task of halakhic discourse, but
Aggadah was intended for everyone who came to the synagogue seeking from their religious traditions sustenance
for daily life.[49] Indeed, even in the academies, a lively
debate over a point of halakhah could be interrupted for
an interlude of aggadic discourse. Through Aggadah, the
rabbis sought to bring scripture into contact with everyday life. Mary Calloway says of Midrash, a literary distilla-
tion of rabbinic Aggadoth dealing with scripture:

> Midrash is first of all a way of interpreting Scripture in
> the context of one's life and interpreting life in the
> context of Scripture. It presupposes a view of Scrip-
> ture which is dynamic rather than static, in which
> Scripture is read as the living word of a living God
> which is addressed to a community living in the
> present.[50]

We err, therefore, if we downplay Aggadah's role
within Jewish communities. For in Aggadah, as one
scholar has written, the rabbis evolved "an ingenious
instrument for deriving guidance from the Torah, for ed-

ucating the people, strengthening their faith, and bolstering their pride and courage."[51] And if, as Lou H. Silberman has suggested, Aggadah both reflected and shaped the ethos—the "sense of existence"—of the Jewish community, then it played no small role in that community's interpretation of Torah, its ethic, as well.[52] Silberman cites, by way of example, the Mishnah's halakhic explication of Deuteronomy 21:18–21a, the case of a disobedient son. According to the biblical text,

> if a man has a wayward and defiant son, who does not heed his father or mother and does not obey them even after they discipline him, his father and mother shall take hold of him and bring him out to the elders of his town at the public place of his community. They shall say to the elders of his town, "This son of ours is disloyal and defiant; he does not heed us. He is a glutton and a drunkard." Thereupon the men of his town shall stone him to death.

This law was part of Torah and could not, of course, be disregarded. Because community ethos resisted its execution, however, the rabbis sought by their halakhic interpretations to limit its applicability, insisting that it referred to a son, but not to a daughter; to a boy, rather than to an adult son; and only to a son who had reached the age of thirteen years and a day, since commandment observance was not encumbent upon males until that age. Moreover, just as the word "son" was constricted in meaning, other words of the law were qualified as well. Clearly, in this case, the community's ethic-shaping ethos was at work, affecting even its interpretation of Written Torah. And that ethos to no small extent not only created, but also was created by, the rabbinical teaching called Aggadah.[53]

Modern readers of the Aggadah (and indeed, of Halakhah as well) are struck by its often quite different hermeneutical principles. Frequently, the rabbis em-

ployed a particular method of aggadic interpretation that
ignored biblical chronology and juxtaposed texts from
quite different periods in Israel's history. If, for example,
a particular text raised a question in their minds, they
could move freely among the biblical books searching for
its answer, so that the words of an eighth-century
prophet could be shown to explain the actions of some-
one who had lived three centuries earlier. All of scripture
is from God, they believed, and scripture interprets scripture. "With aggadic Midrash, as with the legal," Michael
Fishbane writes, "there is the strong presupposition that
Scripture is a seamless web. The exegete is permitted and
encouraged to move back and forth across its surface,
connecting texts and reconnecting them, harmonizing
the contradictory and bringing the seemingly discordant
into patterns of new and surprising concordance."[54]

Moderns may also be surprised by the wealth of legendary embellishments of biblical characters and events
that the rabbis incorporated to delight and instruct their
audiences. Consider, for example, the historical Aggadah
that answers the question posed at the beginning of this
chapter: "Who was King Lemuel, and why did his mother
admonish him?" (Prov. 31:1). According to Jewish tradition, King Lemuel was actually Solomon, son of King David and his wife, Bathsheba.[55] Solomon's mother scolded
him, the rabbis claimed, because she discovered that her
son had neglected his religious responsibilities. On the
very day that he dedicated the temple in Jerusalem (1
Kings 8:1–66), Solomon married the daughter of Pharaoh, king of Egypt. Their wedding night revelry kept him
awake far too long; the next morning, the king slept in.
Because he kept the key to the temple beneath his pillow,
however, no one could enter the sanctuary; and the
morning sacrifice was delayed. "Thereupon his mother
came and tied him—the king!—to a post and delivered
the following lecture to him,"[56] urging that he not spend
too much time in the harem (vs. 2–3), avoid strong drink

(vs. 4–7), and champion the rights of the poor and needy (vs. 8–9). The following poem about the accomplished woman could be interpreted as a continuation of her speech—an attempt to draw a grim contrast between what a wife should be and the foreign woman her son married.[57]

While this legend is certainly entertaining, its didactic intent should not be missed. If even the great King Solomon needed instruction to avoid life's pitfalls and to care for the downtrodden, how much more the young people who learned this legend from their elders. Indeed, the Aggadoth invariably appear for a purpose: to shape moral character; to disclose some deeper meaning of the text; to stimulate the religious imagination; to bring—again, we remember Fishbane's words—"the seemingly discordant into patterns of new and surprising concordance."

An aggadic passage taken from *Midrash Rabbah* illustrates the rabbis' desire to illuminate even the briefest of texts by using scripture to interpret scripture.[58] Our passage is an interpretation of the words, "Then sang Moses," part of the introduction to the "Song of the Sea" (Exod. 15:1–18). This song was sung after YHWH delivered Israel from Pharaoh's soldiers at the Red Sea following the exodus from Egypt.[59] Note that in *Midrash Rabbah* the biblical text under discussion is printed in capital letters, the commentary is printed in regular type, and additional scriptural passages cited both to support and to be illuminated by the Midrash are printed in italics.

Another explanation of THEN SANG MOSES. It is written, *She openeth her mouth with wisdom; and the law of kindness is on her tongue* (Prov. XXXI, 26). From the day when God created the world until the Israelites stood near the sea, no one save Israel sang unto God. He created Adam, yet he did not utter Song; He delivered Abraham from the fiery furnace and from the kings,[60] and he did not utter Song; Isaac, also when saved from the knife, did not utter Song, nor did Jacob when he escaped alive from the angel, from Esau and from the men of Shechem. As soon, however, as Israel came to the Sea, which was divided for them, they uttered Song before God, as it says, THEN SANG MOSES AND THE CHILDREN OF ISRAEL. This is the meaning of, "*She openeth her mouth with wisdom.*" God said: "I have been waiting for these."[61]

In this passage, a verse from our acrostic poem about the accomplished woman unlocks the meaning of Exodus 15:1. When Israel speaks for the first time (for the exodus was surely the birth of the people Israel), she does what other biblical heroes failed to do: She opens her mouth with wisdom—that is, the rabbis said, with a song of praise for her God. Moreover, God both anticipates and enjoys her singing.[62] Of course, no modern critic would think to connect these two quite disparate texts in such fashion.[63] By pairing them, however, these early teachers emphasized both Israel's ongoing obligation to praise God and the Lord's delight in Israel's praise. In a footnote to our Midrash, we learn that a later commentator discerned even greater significance in the rabbis' linking of these two passages. He noted that the next verse in the acrostic poem begins with the words, "She oversees the activities of her household." This he took to mean that God, like the accomplished woman, "carefully regarded Israel's footsteps."[64]

Like the Mishnah and the Talmuds, *Midrash Rabbah* is not the work of a single individual. On the contrary, it preserves the interpretations of generations of rabbis. In subsequent centuries, however, great commentators like Abraham Ibn Ezra (eleventh century C.E.) and Rashi (eleventh to twelfth centuries) produced commentaries on a number of biblical books. We shall refer to such works, as well as to the insights of more contemporary Jewish scholars, in the following chapters.

Feminist Perspectives on the Bible

The women whose perspectives are cited in this book are primarily specialists trained in the critical methods of modern biblical scholarship. They are familiar with historical-critical, social science, and literary approaches; and they use one or more of them in their work. Why, then, is a separate section of this chapter devoted to feminist perspectives on the Bible? The answer to this question lies in the straightforward admission by feminists and womanists[65] that their analyses of biblical texts are not a priori disinterested. Like the ancient rabbis, whose aggadic interpretations of scripture had a purpose—to shape, define, enrich, and strengthen their faith communities—these feminists have an agenda: to interpret the Bible in the service of women, whose lives have historically been enriched but also constricted by scripture and its interpreters. True, feminism has been criticized for its advocacy position by scholars who insist that the only worthwhile scholarship is "objective" scholarship. Feminists respond, however, that all interpretations—theological, historical, sociological, and so on—are influenced to some degree by the interpreter's own conscious and unconscious biases and agendas,[66] and, as Mary Ann Tolbert observes, "to assert that all scholarship is advocacy is not . . . to chart new ground and invite anarchy. It is only to admit honestly what the case has been and still is. The criteria of public evidence, logical argument, reasonable hypotheses and intellectual sophistication still adjudicate acceptable and unacceptable positions."[67]

The Diversity of Feminist Scholarship

Before proceeding, it is important to clarify what we mean by "feminist interpreters" of the Bible. The word "feminist" evokes for some readers the stereotypical image of an abrasive woman, angry at both God and men. It is true that, for the most part, feminists believe modern society is modeled on a "pattern of dominance-submission, which includes political, economic, and social as well as theological dimensions."[68] Moreover, many feminists seek through their scholarship to play a role in changing that pattern by transforming the social structures that oppress women and other subordinated groups. We should not assume, however, that all feminists share the same presuppositions and point of view or work toward exactly the same goals.

In a recent article, Carolyn Osiek has identified five different feminist hermeneutics, or interpretive approaches to scripture, each of which has devotees among contemporary women.[69] At one extreme, says Osiek, are the loyalists: women who affirm that the Bible is the word of God which, by definition, cannot be oppressive. Understood correctly, these women insist, scripture reveals God's perfect plan for human coexistence. If the Bible appears to sanction oppression, "then the mistake lies with the interpreter and interpretive tradition, not with the text."[70]

At the opposite extreme stands the rejectionist perspective. According to this view both the Bible and the Judeo-Christian traditions it represents are "hopelessly sinful, corrupt, and irredeemable" because they are intrinsically patriarchal and therefore inevitably oppressive for women and others who are not part of the dominant group.[71] Feminists of this stripe, Mary Daly among them, have severed their connections with the Bible and so are no longer part of the ongoing dialogue embodied, for example, in the following chapters of this book.

Between these two extremes, however, one finds several other approaches. Revisionists, Osiek says, are feminists who (unlike the rejectionists) are unwilling to abandon the Bible, but who (unlike the loyalists) believe that it bears the marks of the patriarchal societies from which it came. On the one hand, these feminists seek to identify and challenge the Bible's androcentric orientation, suppression of women's contributions to history, images of violence against women, and so on. On the other hand, they emphasize those biblical texts that present women and female imagery in a favorable light.

The fourth approach, a sublimationist hermeneutic, searches out and exalts the "eternal feminine" in biblical symbolism. Here, Osiek observes, the basic premise "is the otherness of the feminine as manifested especially in feminine imagery and symbolism in human culture. As Other, the feminine operates by its own principles and rules, which are totally distinct from those of the male realm . . . and any substantial crossing over in sex roles is against nature."[72] Followers of this approach focus upon Israelite-Jewish feminine imagery for Torah, Wisdom, Jerusalem, and the Shekinah ("God's presence").[73] Within the Christian tradition, they may glorify images of the church as Christ's bride and the symbolism surrounding Mary.

Finally, the liberationist feminist approach attracts scholars whose broader orientation is to liberation theology and who work for the emancipation of women and other subordinate groups, "so that all human persons can be for each other partners and equals in the common task."[74] For advocates of this position, the Bible's central revelatory message is humanity's liberation. In response to that message, these feminists seek to participate through their scholarship in the beginning of the fulfillment of God's just and liberating reign.

The Roots of Contemporary Feminist Interpretation

Earlier, we noted that the historical-critical method has been widely applied to biblical literature for approximately two and half centuries. The Jews have been interpreting their scripture for more than two and a half millennia. Some readers may think, however, that feminist interpretations of the Bible are the product of only the past two and a half decades or so. This is not the case. The sublimationist approach's roots, for example, go deep into the early and medieval mystical traditions of both Jews and Christians. But advocates for the four other hermeneutical stances Osiek has identified can be found, as well, among American women living prior to the twentieth century.[75]

Consider, for example, the two extreme positions: loyalist and rejectionist. On the one hand, Sarah Grimké, a nineteenth century Quaker active in the abolition of slavery movement, shared with contemporary loyalists a belief that biased (male) exegesis, and not the Bible itself, was responsible for biblical interpretations resulting in the subjection of women. In 1837, she urged young women with a gift for languages to learn Hebrew and Greek in order to interpret scripture for themselves.[76] On the other hand, Elizabeth Cady Stanton concluded that patriarchy was endemic to the Judeo-Christian tradition. She insisted that "[one] cannot twist out of the Old Testament or the New Testament [in plain English] a message of justice, liberty, or equality from God to the women of the nineteenth century."[77] Although Stanton, editor and frequent commentator for *The Woman's Bible* (published between 1895 and 1898), did not abandon scripture altogether, her views presaged the rejectionist's conclusion that the Bible is, for women, irredeemably oppressive.

For their part, revisionists and liberationist feminists can claim Frances Willard (1839–1898) among their foremothers. Willard, who served for years as president of the Women's Christian Temperance Union, would not relinquish the biblical tradition. She recognized, however, that certain scriptural passages could not be purged of oppressive elements, even at the hands of "objective" (i.e., female) interpreters; and she argued that such texts should be critiqued "in the light of the freeing activity of Jesus Christ," who was "women's emancipator."[78] None of these approaches, therefore, is an altogether "new thing on earth,"[79] an invention of the late twentieth century.

The Tasks of Feminist Biblical Scholarship

Some people believe that feminist biblical scholars are preoccupied solely with the issue of inclusive language, that is, language that does not use masculine nouns (e.g., "mankind") and pronouns that generically refer to both males and females. This is scarcely surprising, since the press has seized upon the inclusive language debate but has said little about other feminist concerns. Women have indeed addressed this issue, believing that language not only is shaped by, but also shapes, thought. If, for example, the word "man" can be used generically to represent all human beings, but "woman" cannot, then by our speech we suggest that men are somehow more than women—that men are normative in a way that women are not.

Feminists also have noted the importance of the language we use to speak about God. While the image of God as "father" has a biblical basis, it certainly does not exhaust the Bible's many ways of addressing, and imaging, the deity.[80] Hence, scholars like Sallie McFague warn against the idolatry of sanctioning only one image of God—a step the biblical authors did not take.[81] Liberationist feminists further remind us that imaging God exclusively as "father" has serious social implications for females and subordinated males. Rosemary Radford Ruether, for example, observes that

Most images of God in religions are modelled after the ruling class of society. In biblical religion the image of

God is that of patriarchal Father above the visible created world, who relates to Israel as his "wife" and
"children" in the sense of creatures totally dependent
on his will, owing him unquestioning obedience. This
image allows the king and patriarchal class to relate to
women, children, and servants through the same
model of domination and dependency.[82]

Despite the seriousness of these issues, however, inclusive
language and imagery are not feminists' sole concern.
Rather, their work is characterized by tremendous diversity, regarding both subject matter and methodology.

Basic to feminist interpretation is a hermeneutic of suspicion. In other words, feminists do not approach a text
with the presupposition that its author(s) have written
disinterested, objective accounts about events "just as
they happened." If ancient Israel's patriarchal social
structures had exercised no influence whatsoever upon
the shapers of Israel's traditions—if women were, in fact,
scarce in ancient Israel (as the paucity of biblical material
about women might, on the face of things, suggest), and
if women's experiences and contributions actually were,
as many narratives present them, limited primarily to
their sexual and reproductive capabilities—then a hermeneutic of suspicion would be unnecessary. As we
noted above, however, feminists and other scholars as
well have become increasingly aware that wholly objective, utterly undistorted accounts and reconstructions of
history were as impossible for ancient Israelite authors as
they are for contemporary writers.[83] The biblical authors
and editors were certainly influenced, consciously and
unconsciously, by their environments.[84] Their patriarchal
orientation explains, feminists argue, the limited, often
stereotypical depictions of women in biblical literature as
well as the circumscribed arena of activity to which they
are, for the most part, relegated.[85]

Some feminists seek, therefore, to retrieve biblical stories about women from their patriarchal settings and to

examine them without presupposing that their characters actually lived on the periphery of Israel's society.[86] Consider, for example, the story of Huldah, the prophetess asked by King Josiah's priests to verify the contents of a law scroll discovered in the Jerusalem temple. Apart from identifying her as a prophetess, the Bible tells us nothing about her, save the names of her husband, her father-in-law, and his father (thereby establishing her husband's patriarchal pedigree). Modern scholars have sometimes asked why this woman was consulted when no less a prophet than Jeremiah was living at the time. Feminist scholars point out, however, that the narrator appears to accept the existence of an influential female intermediary as a matter of course. This suggests that powerful women may have been more numerous in ancient Israel than the biblical record suggests.[87]

Feminists are cautious, however, about accepting at face value every female role model proffered by biblical authors. Recognizing that rhetoric, skillfully wielded, can exert an enormous impact on readers, they search out literary strategies by which narrators commend to their readers—male and female—certain values and points of view.

Feminist interpreters also examine biblical stories about violence against women, as well as the many appearances of misogynist female imagery that, we must assume, influenced to some degree the attitudes of biblical men and women toward women. Many of these texts—the story of Jephthah's unnamed daughter (Judg. 11:1–40), the rape and murder of a Levite's unnamed concubine (Judg. 19:1–30),[88] and the grisly description of YHWH's treatment of Samaria and Jerusalem, personified as females (e.g., Ezekiel 16, 23)—are painful and are rarely the topic of sermons or religious education curricula.[89] Feminists remember these victims, however, and lift up their stories and images so that the savagery committed against females is confronted, not forgotten. In a world where each day's headlines include new incidents of rape, physical abuse, and murder, feminists insist that these biblical stories are far from just "ancient history."[90]

Many feminists recognize, however, that despite the effects of oppressive social structures upon biblical literature, the Bible "is not only a book that has justified slavery, economic exploitation, and sexual oppression; it is also a book that has informed liberation, the infinite worth of the individual, and the call to fight against evil."[91] Ruether, for example, believes that the core of the Bible's central, liberating message can be found in ancient Israel's prophetic tradition:

> In the prophetic perspective, God speaks through the prophet or prophetess as critic, rather than sanctifier, of the status quo. God's will is revealed as standing in judgment upon the injustices of the way society is being conducted, especially by the wealthy and powerful. This critique of society includes a critique of religion. The spokesperson of God denounces the way in which religion is misused to countenance injustice and to turn away the eyes of the pious from the poor. In the words of Amos 5:21, 24, "I hate, I despite your feasts, and I take no delight in your solemn assemblies. . . . But let justice roll down like waters, and righteousness like an everflowing stream."[92]

True, the prophet Amos does not mention women explicitly. Moreover, Israel's prophetic literature contains some of scripture's most misogynist imagery.[93] Ruether insists, however, that once the prophetic critique of unjust structures—and the religious justifications for those structures—is freed from its cultural distortions, it can serve as a yardstick against which even the prophets' own sexism can be measured and judged.

As Ruether's quotation from Amos 5:21, 24 indicates, feminists' interests are not confined to texts that refer explicitly to women or contain female imagery. Rather, they are investigating the whole range of biblical literature. Moreover, their critiques extend beyond the Bible to its interpreters. Jewish women are exploring patriarchy's effects not only within the biblical corpus but also in the interpretive literature of the rabbis.[94] Jewish and Christian feminists are questioning many of the presuppositions undergirding conceptual models traditionally used by biblical scholars to illumine the world of ancient Israel. Historically, for example, specialists have used dualistic models that divided reality into opposing pairs: male/female, physical/spiritual, good/bad, and so on. Applied to a subject like the history of Israelite religion, a dualistic model places Yahwistic religion at one pole and Canaanite religion at another.[95] Of course, the biblical narrators spoke in just this way, as if the two religious systems were clearly distinguishable and utterly unreconcilable from the outset. In their view (adopted uncritically by some biblical scholars), Israelites whose religious practices fell somewhere between these two poles were willfully abandoning "pure" Yahwism for idolatry. Feminists, however, have questioned the validity of historical reconstructions based upon such dualistic models, arguing that we understand the historical relationship between Yahwism and Canaanite religion better if we adopt models that allow for "shifting movement in which the new is slowly interwoven with the larger fabric of older, continued experience."[96] Indeed, feminists are also among those contemporary scholars who question the adequacy of our traditional reconstructions and understandings of Canaanite religious practices.[97]

These few paragraphs by no means exhaust the work of feminist biblical scholarship. They are, however, suggestive of the broad range of interests, questions and approaches among contemporary feminist interpreters of scripture. In the following chapters, you will have an opportunity to enjoy some of the fruits of their labors.

Conclusion

This chapter has sketched the interpretive approaches utilized by our three major constituencies—critical specialists, rabbinical interpreters, and critical feminist scholars. My purpose has been to prepare readers for chapters 2 through 5, where insights from these groups inform our telling of biblical women's stories. In what follows, my use of these diverse resources is eclectic, not systematic. Rarely do I bring all three perspectives to bear on a single text at a single point. More often, I have judged when a text raises an issue best addressed by critical scholarship, where the rabbis have contributed insights that simply must be shared, and when a feminist interpreter has put her finger on some crucial and previously overlooked dimension of the story. My interweaving of perspectives is not always balanced, in the sense that I have not tried to ensure that every chapter contains 33 percent of each interpretive approach. Rather, I have allowed one perspective or another to predominate at points if, in my judgment, its contribution has been especially important or insightful.

Readers should be aware that I do not intend to place the perspectives of these three constituencies in competition with each other, to render judgments about each individual contribution, or to end the book by declaring one constituency the "winner." Neither do I attempt consistently to bring these three perspectives into dialogue with each other. To be sure, there are points along the way where one perspective is considered in light of another's insights into a text. However, a sustained conversation among these diverse perspectives would be difficult, if not impossible, to maintain, given the enormous differences separating, for example, modern practitioners of social science approaches to a text and the early rabbis, with their interpretive strategies and goals. Rather, I leave to readers the task of discerning the questions and concerns that motivate different interpreters, of judging the value of their insights, and of using those insights to inform and enrich their own perspectives. My hope is that the following chapters will enhance immeasurably your relationship with the four accomplished biblical women whose stories you are about to read.

Notes

1. In an acrostic poem, each verse begins with a word that starts with successive letters of the alphabet. Hence, the first word of Prov. 31:10 begins with an *aleph,* the first word of v. 11 begins with a *bet,* and so on through the twenty-two letters of the Hebrew alphabet.

2. Despite the claim in v. 16 that the accomplished woman "plants a vineyard by her own labors," the great eleventh-century commentator, Ibn Ezra, insisted that she simply arranged for the planting to be done, since doing so herself would be unseemly. See Scherman, *Zemiroth,* p. 54.

3. I am indebted to my student Eileen Noyes-Verchereau for this insight.

4. The order in which I tell these stories violates biblical chronology, which would place Ruth's story after the Sarah and Hagar narratives, but before the book of Esther. According to my arrangement, the stories of Sarah and Hagar are preceded by the tale of a foreign woman (a Moabite princess, according to the rabbis) who leaves her homeland to dwell in Israel and are followed by the story of a Jewish woman who becomes queen in a foreign court.

5. What has been said here is equally true of New Testament scholars. We shall, however, confine our discussion and examples to the Hebrew Bible.

6. Most Jewish scholars, of course, already knew Hebrew.

7. *Assertio omnium articulum M. Lutheri per Bullam Leonis X. novissimam damnatorum* (1519, WA, VII, 97). The translation is by Werner Georg Kümmel in *The New Testament: The History of the Investigation of Its Problems,* tr. S. McLean Gilmour and Howard C. Kee (Nashville and New York: Abingdon, 1972), p. 22, as cited in Krentz, *The Historical-Critical Method,* p. 8.

8. Brevard Childs argues that the Bible's silence on such issues is intentional, not coincidental. In his *Introduction to the Old Testament as Scripture,* Childs writes, " . . . the identity of the canonical editors has been consciously obscured, and the only signs of an ongoing history are found in the multi-layered text of scripture itself. The shape of the canon directs the reader's attention to the sacred writings rather than to their editors" (p. 59).

9. The word Pentateuch ("five scrolls") is commonly used by biblical scholars to refer to the first five books of the Bible—Genesis, Exodus, Leviticus, Numbers, and Deuteronomy.

10. Torah ("teaching," "law") is sometimes used among Jews to refer to all their scripture. More frequently, however, it has the sense intended here—that is, it refers to the first five books of the Hebrew Bible. So defined, it becomes a synonym of "Pentateuch." For the distinction between Written Torah and Oral Torah, see the section "Jewish Interpretation of Scripture."

11. Spinoza, *The Chief Works of Benedict de Spinoza,* p. 124. Spinoza cites Ibn Ezra's eliptical remarks on p. 121.

12. For example, the mountain to which Moses and the Israelites journeyed after the exodus is called Sinai in some texts, Horeb in others.

13. According to Gen. 7:2, God told Noah to bring onto the ark seven pairs of every clean animal and one pair of every unclean animal. In 7:15, however, only one pair of every kind of living creature enters the ark.

14. YHWH (called the Tetragrammaton ["four letters"]) are the four consonants in the personal name of Israel's God, Yahweh. During the post-exilic period, a tradition arose within Judaism that the divine name was too sacred to pronounce. Jewish readers therefore substituted a title, such as *Adonay* ("Lord") when they came upon YHWH in the biblical text. In most English translations of the Bible, it is common practice to render YHWH as "Lord." The Jerusalem Bible, however, retains "Yahweh." Because source criticism was developed primarily by German scholars, the first letter of the German spelling, "Jahweh," was used to designate this, the oldest of the pentateuchal sources.

15. B.C.E. stands for "before the Common Era." Its more common equivalent is B.C., "before Christ." C.E. stands for

"Common Era." Its more common equivalent is A.D., "anno Domini" ("in the year of our Lord"). Our usage intends to be more inclusive of Jewish as well as Christian readers.

16. See Wellhausen's *Prolegomena to the History of Ancient Israel.* The material in the *Prolegomena* first appeared in 1878 under the title *Geschichte Israels I.*

17. A minority view holds that the "Yahwist," that is, the author-editor who linked Israel's patriarchal and matriarchal traditions to the pentateuchal themes of exodus, wandering in the wilderness, covenant-making at Sinai, and entrance into the promised land, should be dated to the late pre-exilic or exilic period (seventh to sixth centuries B.C.E.).

18. On the Old Epic narrative, see Anderson, *Understanding the Old Testament,* pp. 151–180. Gottwald provides a compact statement of source criticism's criteria and evidence in *The Hebrew Bible,* pp. 11–13.

19. Unless otherwise noted, scriptural translations in this book are from *Tanakh.*

20. Note, too, the difference between *striking* the Nile (Old Epic) and stretching a staff *over* the waters (P).

21. Its internal development may be more difficult to follow, however, because the poet is, at least to some degree, constrained by the requirement that a particular line begin with a specific letter.

22. According to traditional practice, a husband recites this poem to his wife before dinner on Sabbath eve.

23. A pericope (a Greek term meaning "a cutting all around") is a discrete literary unit, e.g., a proverb, poem, or parable. Determining the beginning and end of a pericope is the first task of form criticism.

24. Many of the existing ancient texts from Israel's world are collected and translated in Pritchard, ed., *Ancient Near Eastern Texts.*

25. Contemporary archaeologists rightly argue that their discipline should not be undertaken simply in the service of substantiating the Bible's witness to events in Israel's history. See Dever, "Syro-Palestinian and Biblical Archaeology," pp. 31–74.

26. Both of these approaches are tremendously complex. What follows is only the briefest of introductions to each field.

27. See Wilson, *Sociological Approaches to the Old Testament.*

28. Gottwald, *The Hebrew Bible,* p. 26.

29. Ibid., p. 28.

30. See Overholt, *Channels of Prophecy: The Social Dynamics of Prophetic Activity,* pp. 6–11.

31. See Wilson, *Prophecy and Society in Ancient Israel* and, more recently, Overholt, *Channels of Prophecy.*

32. Gottwald, *The Hebrew Bible,* p. 22.

33. This does not mean, however, that all literary critics ignore history, for an understanding of the cultural, and especially the literary, milieu of a work can shed a great deal of light on how it functions. However, the emphasis differs: Here, the critic uses history to illumine the text; there, the critic uses the text as a window on history.

34. Alter, "Introduction to the Old Testament," p. 25.

35. Literary methods differ primarily in their understanding of authors, texts, and readers. Where does meaning lie: in the author's intent, in the text, or in the readers, who bring to the text their own unique presuppositions, knowledge, and point of view? See chapter 2 in John A. Darr, " 'Glorified in the Presence of Kings.' "

36. Phyllis Trible, whose work will be cited frequently in the following chapters, uses a literary method called "rhetorical criticism" to enrich our awareness of the biblical narrator's skill. Students frequently remark that after having read a narrative through Trible's eyes they never read it in quite the same way again. See, for example, her *Texts of Terror.* Rhetorical criticism is indebted to the New Literary Criticism practiced by critics such as Northrop Frye and Wayne Booth. But it also has links both to form criticism (since it attends to the shape of texts), to redaction criticism (which examines texts in their final or near-final form), and to forms of canonical criticism that emphasize the final, canonical shape of the biblical text.

37. In addition to *Torah* (Genesis–Deuteronomy), Hebrew scripture contains *Nebi'im* ("Prophets") and *Kethubim* ("Writings"). The Prophets portion is subdivided into "Former Prophets" (Joshua–II Kings) and "Latter Prophets" (Isaiah, Jeremiah, and Ezekiel, as well as the "Book of the Twelve"— Hosea, Joel, Amos, Obadiah, Jonah, Micah, Nahum, Habakkuk, Zephaniah, Haggai, Zechariah, and Malachi). The Writings include Psalms, Job, Proverbs, Ruth, Song of Songs, Ecclesiastes (also called Qoheleth), Lamentations, Esther, Daniel, Ezra, Nehemiah, and Chronicles.

38. Compare Deut. 16:3–4 and Deut. 16:8.

39. Does Exod. 21:22–23, for example, speak of harm done to a woman, or to her fetus?

40. *Encyclopaedia Judaica,* s.v. "Oral Law."

41. Sefer Ha-Mitzvoth, Introduction (II, 361), quoted in Twersky, *Introduction to the Code of Maimonides (Mishneh Torah),* pp. 26 and 99.

42. That is, the period after the Babylonian exile, which ended in approximately 538 B.C.E.

43. The Mishnah is divided into six sections, called *Sedarim* ("Orders"). These Orders are divided into Tractates, each of which is further divided into chapters. The six Orders of the Mishnah are *Zeraim* ("Seeds"), *Moed* ("Festival"), *Nashim* ("Women"), *Nezikin* ("Damages"), *Kodashim* ("Holy Things"), and *Teharoth* ("Purifications").

44. The rabbinical writings themselves, the literary remains of sects like the Essene community at Qumran, and New Testament authors testify to sharp differences among Jews about correct religious practice as well as about how scripture should be interpreted in order that its "true" meaning might be discerned and followed.

45. "Exegetical" comes from the noun "exegesis" (Greek, meaning "explanation," "interpretation") and refers to the systematic interpretation of texts.

46. This statement does not, of course, rule out the possibility that some—perhaps many—of the Pharisees' exegetical and practical traditions were deeply rooted in the history of Israelite/Jewish religious observance. On this historical reconstruction of Oral Torah's origins, see Neusner, "Scripture and Mishnah," pp. 64–85.

47. Corre, "The Mishnah," in *Understanding the Talmud,* p. 9.

48. Because the four stories discussed in this book are not legal texts, the rabbinical materials cited are aggadic, rather than halakhic.

49. Of course, observance of Halakhah was required of Jews whether they studied in the academies or not. But while the debate over halakhic judgments was complex, technical, and not undertaken by all Jewish men, Aggadah was intended for the layperson as well as for the rabbis.

50. Calloway, *Sing, O Barren One,* p. 5.

51. *Encyclopaedia Judaica,* s.v. "Aggadah," p. 355. The initials

"E. H." appear on p. 353 of the article, indicating that the section in which this quotation appears was taken from *Encyclopaedia Hebraica*.

52. Silberman, "Aggadah and Halakhah," pp. 223–229.

53. Ibid., pp. 228–231.

54. Fishbane, "Jewish Bible Exegesis," p. 99.

55. The rabbis took King Lemuel's name to mean "upon God." He was identified with Solomon because the latter was said to have based his life "upon God." See Plaut, *The Book of Proverbs*, p. 310.

56. Ibid.

57. Alternatively, the text was understood to be Abraham's eulogy for Sarah. See Scherman, *Zemiroth*, p. 50.

58. *Midrash Rabbah* contains aggadic material on the Pentateuch, plus the five *Megilloth* ("festival scrolls")—Song of Songs, Ruth, Lamentations, Ecclesiastes, and Esther—read in the course of the Jewish liturgical year. The contents of Genesis Rabbah, Leviticus Rabbah, much of Esther Rabbah, and Ruth Rabbah were committed to writing about 400–640 C.E. The midrash on certain late additions to the book of Esther probably dates from the tenth century. See *Encyclopaedia Judaica*, s.v. "Midrash."

59. Many scholars believe that Exod. 15:2–18 was actually Miriam's song, as vs. 20–21 suggest. Childs notes that "the tendency to ascribe an ancient poem to Moses would have taken precedence over Miriam's authorship" (*Exodus*, p. 248).

60. The legendary adventures of Abraham, including his escape from the fiery furnace (compare Dan. 3:1–30) are collected in Ginzberg, *The Legends of the Jews*, vol. 1, pp. 185–308.

61. Exodus (Beshallach) XXIII 4, pp. 281–282.

62. At the same time that the quotation from Proverbs sheds light on Moses and the Israelites, the Midrash adds a new dimension to Prov. 31:26. To the question "What is the true identity of this accomplished woman?" this midrash replies, "She is the newly-delivered Israel, opening her mouth with wisdom and singing God's praise."

63. Perhaps the idea first occurred to the rabbis because the Hebrew word for "song" appears in Exod. 15:1 in its feminine form.

64. Exodus (Beshallach) XXIII 4, p. 282, n. 1. The insight is found in *Maharzu*, a nineteenth-century commentary by Ze'eb

Wolf Einhorn. Note that Einhorn had no difficulty shifting the feminine pronoun's referent from Israel in v. 26 to God in v. 27.

65. Many black women choose to refer to themselves as "womanists," rather than "feminists." The term is from Alice Walker, *In Search of Our Mothers' Gardens,* pp. xi–xii. Walker explains that "womanist" is "from womanish (opposite of 'girlish,' i.e., frivolous, 'irresponsible, not serious'). A black feminist or feminist of color." See Cannon, "The Emergence of Black Feminist Consciousness," pp. 30–40.

66. See, for example, the cogent argument by Fiorenza in "Remembering the Past in Creating the Future," pp. 43–63.

67. Tolbert recognizes that these criteria are themselves problematic, because judgments about what is "logical" or "reasonable" also are subjective. See her discussion in "Defining the Problem," pp. 117–121.

68. Osiek, "The Feminist and the Bible," p. 103.

69. Ibid., pp. 97–104.

70. Ibid., p. 99. Osiek refers readers to two examples of a loyalist hermeneutic at work: Richard and Joyce Boldrey, *Chauvinist or Feminist? Paul's View of Women* and Evelyn and Frank Stagg, *Woman in the World of Jesus.*

71. Osiek, "The Feminist and the Bible," p. 98.

72. Ibid., pp. 101–102.

73. *Torah, Hochmah* ("Wisdom"), and *Shekinah*—like *'îr* (a Hebrew word for "city")—are all feminine nouns. This fact undoubtedly contributed to the development of female imagery (e.g., personification) of these entities and concepts.

74. Ibid., p. 103.

75. These women were lay people, rather than trained biblical scholars. Indeed, Dorothy Bass points out that until the 1960s and '70s, feminist biblical interpretation was undertaken by women outside the guild of critical biblical scholarship. See her historical essay "Women's Studies and Biblical Studies," pp. 6–12, as well as Gifford, "American Women and the Bible," pp. 12–33.

76. Bass, "Women's Studies and Biblical Studies," p. 7.

77. Quoted in Gifford, "American Women and the Bible," p. 30.

78. Gifford, "American Women and the Bible," p. 26. Gifford notes the similarity between Willard's "Bible-precept prin-

ciples" and the identification by Ruether, for example, of the prophets as the Bible's central liberating core.

79. The phrase is from Jer. 31:22 (RSV).

80. See, for example, Trible, *God and the Rhetoric of Sexuality*, pp. 50–56, 60–68; Gruber, "The Motherhood of God in Second Isaiah," pp. 351–359; Bronner, "Gynomorphic Imagery in Exilic Isaiah (40–66)," pp. 71–83; Schmitt, "The Motherhood of God and Zion as Mother," pp. 557–569; Darr, "Like Warrior, Like Woman: Destruction and Deliverance in Isaiah 42:10–17," pp. 560–571.

81. McFague, *Metaphorical Theology*.

82. Reuther, *New Woman-New Earth*, pp. 74–75.

83. Contemporary hermeneutical theory, informed by the findings of depth psychology and the sociology of knowledge, acknowledges that all interpretations, including historical and theological ones, are to some degree advocacy positions.

84. Loyalist feminists will not, for the most part, agree that human factors such as social influences have shaped biblical narrative. They must therefore be bracketed from this discussion.

85. Feminists bring a hermeneutic of suspicion to biblical stories about women, for example, because most of those stories were composed by men and reflect what men thought about women, rather than what women themselves thought.

86. See, for example, Meyers, *Discovering Eve*. Meyers uses archaeological data and social science methods to reconstruct the everyday lives and contributions of Israelite women living prior to the establishment of Israel's monarchy (about 1020 B.C.E.).

87. In her work with the Gospels and the Pauline epistles, Fiorenza discerns evidence for an early Jesus movement that included powerful women and was thoroughly egalitarian. See *In Memory of Her*.

88. Levites were members of the tribe of Levi. According to Israel's ancestral traditions, members of this tribe were descended from, and bore the name of, Jacob and Leah's third son.

89. Trible's book, *Texts of Terror*, includes chapters devoted to Jephthah's daughter and the unnamed concubine.

90. See, for example, Thistlethwaite, "Every Two Minutes," in Russell, *Feminist Interpretation*, pp. 96–107.

91. Tolbert, "Defining the Problem," p. 120.

92. Ruether, "Feminist Interpretation," pp. 117–118.

93. See Setel, "Prophets and Pornography," pp. 86–95.

94. See, for example, Hauptman, "Images of Women in the Talmud," pp. 184–212; and Umansky, "Beyond Androcentrism," pp. 25–35.

95. See Setel, "Feminist Insights and the Question of Method," in Collins, *Feminist Perspectives,* pp. 35–42.

96. Ibid., p. 40.

97. See, for example, Hackett, "Can A Sexist Model Liberate Us?" pp. 65–76; Leith, "Verse and Reverse," pp. 95–108; Bird, "To Play the Harlot," pp. 75–94; and Adler, "The Background for the Metaphor of Covenant as Marriage in the Hebrew Bible."

"More than Seven Sons": Critical, Rabbinical, and Feminist Perspectives on Ruth

"R. Ze'ira said: This scroll [of Ruth] tells us nothing either of cleanliness or of uncleanliness, either of prohibition or permission. For what purpose then was it written? To teach how great is the reward of those who do deeds of kindness."[1]

Who Was Ruth?

Imagine for a moment that you are able to journey back to the ancient Israel of "biblical times."[2] Walking through the streets of Jerusalem, you strike up a conversation with a fellow pedestrian; and as you talk about this impressive city, home of the royal Davidic family, you happen to mention Ruth. "Who is Ruth?" he asks. You begin to share her story, but your companion repeatedly interrupts you with incredulous remarks:

"*Who* was Ruth? Ruth was a *Moabite*?[3] Well, that's not good! Since those ancient days when Moses led our ancestors through the desert, and the king of Moab hired Balaam to curse them, hatred has existed between Moabites and Israelites.[4] Remember the horrible fate promised them by the prophet Jeremiah: 'The doom of Moab is coming close, His downfall is approaching swiftly. . . . Moab is shamed and dismayed; Howl and cry aloud! Tell at the Arnon[5] that Moab is ravaged!'[6] Isaiah, too, foretold the demise of the hated Moabites, saying 'For the hand of the Lord will rest on this mountain, and Moab shall be trodden down in his place, as straw is trodden down in a dung pit.'[7] Oh yes, and remember what God's great servant, Moses, said concerning Moabites? 'No Ammonite or Moabite shall be admitted into the congregation of the Lord; none of their descendants, even in the tenth generation, shall ever be admitted into the congregation of the Lord.'[8] That's what he said! No, whoever this Ruth may be, nothing good ever came out of Moab.

"*What's* that you say? Ruth was a Moabitess? A woman? Worse still! If this were a man, he might at least become a mighty warrior, a mercenary fighting in Israel's army like Uriah, the Hittite, Bathsheba's . . . uh, unfortunate husband. If he were shrewd and ambitious, he might become a prosperous tradesman, leading caravans through the desert and bringing to the land of Israel spices and cloth, silver and cedar, ivory and gold. But a woman? What good can come of a woman—unless, of course, she is a proper wife who bears many strong sons for her husband.

"Oh, but you *cannot* mean it! Ruth was barren; and her husband died, leaving her a widow? That settles it, then. Nothing can come of this Ruth woman, this Moabitess, this sinful creature whom YHWH has punished with barrenness,[9] and who is alone in the world without a husband to provide shelter, protection, and social standing within the community. She is less than nothing. I cannot understand how you even know her name."

As you finish your story, however, your new friend responds, "Yes, now I understand. You know her name because she is the ancestress of David, our mighty king, the beloved shepherd boy singled out by God and established upon the throne here in Jerusalem. David, whose descendants shall rule God's people forever. David, from whose line will come the Messiah. That is why you know about Ruth. And that is why we must continually sing praise to the Lord, the Holy One in our midst, who acts in unexpected ways through persons we dismiss as 'the least of these.' "

Perspectives on the Story of Ruth

Of all the books within the Bible, only two short scrolls—Ruth and Esther—are named for women.[10] Yet these two stories and the women whose names they bear have enjoyed tremendous popularity throughout the centuries. We shall return to Esther in chapter 5. At present, our subject is Ruth the Moabitess, great-grandmother of King David and ancestress of Jesus of Nazareth (see Matt. 1:5–6, RSV).

People bring many different questions and concerns to the book of Ruth and, not surprisingly, go away with a variety of answers and interpretations. For example, first-time readers, ancient and modern, enjoy Ruth for its delightful characters and plot; they read to discover how things will "turn out." Contemporary biblical scholars relish a good story, too, but they study Ruth for other reasons as well—e.g., for the light it can shed on such ancient Israelite societal practices as land redemption and levirate marriage.[11]

For centuries following its composition, the rabbis studied the Ruth scroll, coaxing forth its mysteries and finding answers to questions we might never even think to ask. Often, their aggadic interpretations are startlingly insightful; frequently, they are intentionally humorous. Always, they remind us that biblical interpretation began long before the onset of modern critical scholarship.

Not surprisingly, contemporary feminist and womanist interpreters of scripture have been drawn to Ruth as well. Like the rabbis, these specialists often pose unanticipated questions. And again, new questions yield new insights—fresh ways of thinking about an old, old story.

The Setting of Ruth

In Hebrew Bibles, the book of Ruth appears within the third and last section of the canon, the "Writings."[12] Appropriately placed between the book of Proverbs and the Song of Songs, Ruth is preceded by a poetic description of the accomplished woman in Proverbs 31:10–31 and followed by the romantic, sometimes erotic, love songs attributed to Solomon, the Israelite king who was as renowned for his harem as he was for his wisdom.[13] In most English Bibles, however, Ruth follows the book of Judges. The reason for this arrangement is not difficult to understand, since Ruth 1:1 places the story "in the days when the judges ruled" (RSV).[14]

Readers of Ruth, however, find themselves in a world quite different from that encountered in the book of Judges. The latter work ends in a morass of savagery and self-indulgence. A Levite's concubine is gang-raped in the Benjaminite city of Gibeah (Judges 19). Later, her body is dismembered and the pieces distributed among the other Israelite tribes as a grisly call to war.[15] Thirsty for revenge, the men of Israel set out to defeat the tribe of Benjamin, eventually slaughtering 25,100 Benjaminite warriors (20:35). Yet with their victory comes remorse, because the zeal of intertribal conflict threatens that "one tribe must now be missing from Israel" (21:3). The problem is resolved in horrific fashion. Members of another Israelite tribe, settled at Jabesh-gilead, are slaughtered, save for four hundred young virgins. These women are kidnapped and given to the remaining sons of Benjamin in order that their tribe "not be blotted out of Israel" (21:17). And when these four hundred are not enough, the remaining Benjaminites are given permission by the other tribes to kidnap young women from the settlement at Shiloh when they go out into the vineyards to dance. True indeed are the words with which the book of Judges ends: "In those days there was no king in Israel; everyone did as he pleased" (21:25).

Yes, the social situation presupposed in Ruth differs considerably from that found throughout much of the book of Judges. Ruth's story has no murderers, villains, or acts of treachery. The people of Bethlehem suffer from famine, but not from social discord. Moreover, one does not find in Ruth the supranormal events that appear within the book of Judges (e.g., 6:20–22; 13:19–21) and elsewhere in our Hebrew scriptures. The sun does not stand still for Ruth; no one is swallowed by a fish. YHWH does not appear as a divine warrior, ensuring Israelite victory over its foes. Rather, God works behind the scenes through characters who triumph over adversity by acts of extraordinary devotion and initiative.

Scene One

Our story begins on a tragic note. Famine afflicts the land of Judah, forcing a Bethlehemite named Elimelech, his wife, Naomi, and their two sons, Mahlon and Chilion, to migrate to Moab. There, Elimelech dies. Mahlon and Chilion marry Moabite women, Orpah and Ruth; but after a decade, both sons perish as well. Widowed and bereaved of her children, Naomi decides that the time has come to return home, since the famine there has ended.

Accompanied by her daughters-in-law, Naomi begins her journey. Soon, however, she strongly encourages each woman to return to "her mother's house" (Ruth 1:8). After all, she has no hope of bearing future husbands for them. At length, Orpah dries her tears and obeys her mother-in-law. But Ruth steadfastly refuses to return to "her people and her gods" (1:15). "Do not urge me to leave you, to turn back and not follow you," she entreats Naomi. "For wherever you go, I will go; wherever you lodge, I will lodge; your people shall be my people, and your God my God. Where you die, I will die, and there I will be buried. Thus and more may the Lord do to me[16] if anything but death parts me from you" (1:16–18).

In the face of such resolve, Naomi relents; and the two women continue on their way to Bethlehem. Arriving in the city, they generate considerable excitement and curiosity among the townswomen, who gather around to see their old friend. "Can this be Naomi?" they exclaim (1:19). The old woman's response gives full voice to the bitterness of her experience and introduces important themes that will recur throughout the remainder of the story: "Do not call me Naomi,"[17] she replied. "Call me Mara,[18] for Shaddai[19] has made my lot very bitter. I went away full, and the Lord has brought me back empty.[20] How can you call me Naomi, when the Lord has dealt harshly with me, when Shaddai has brought misfortune upon me?" (1:20).

For want of food (lack of seed), Naomi, "full" of family, left Bethlehem, a name that means "House of Bread." Now her homeland is fertile once more, but she is empty, since both spouse and seed (progeny) have perished. Will the Lord make her full again?[21] The conclusion of Scene One suggests that there is hope for her future, for we read in verse 22b that the two widows arrive in Bethlehem "at the beginning of the barley harvest."[22]

Rabbinical Interpretations of Scene One

We must interrupt our story at this point to consider some of what the rabbis had to say about events narrated thus far. The trials of Elimelech and his family generated considerable interest among the rabbis, indeed, and not a few questions—queries that were neither asked nor answered by the ancient author of Ruth. They wondered, for example, why both Elimelech and his two sons suffered tragic, premature deaths. Modern biblical scholars point out that the sudden loss of family members at the beginning of a story is a literary convention; tragedy becomes the opportunity for the subsequent plot.[23] Job suffers a similar loss, for example, in Job 1:18–19. In the rabbis' opinion, however, such calamity could only be understood as YHWH's just punishment for some heinous transgression. But for what offense were the male members of this family destroyed?

The rabbis discerned a clue to Elimelech's sin in his name, which may be taken to mean "to me shall kingship come." A proud and boastful individual, Elimelech was personally unaffected by the famine, they claimed, for his personal wealth was sufficient to provide for his family's needs. Nevertheless, he left his homeland in order to avoid the responsibility of caring for less fortunate neighbors.[24] Moreover, Elimelech compounded his sinfulness by choosing Moab as his destination, a direct violation of Moses' order that "You shall never concern yourself with [Moab's] welfare or benefit as long as you live" (Deut. 23:7).[25]

His sons, Mahlon and Chilion, likewise were struck

down in untimely fashion on account of sin. Their transgression, however, was marrying foreign women.[26] The
rabbis insisted, moreover, that their brides were not just
any foreigners. No, they were princesses, daughters of
Eglon, King of Moab, who offered his children to
Elimelech's sons after they prospered and became famous in their newly adopted land.[27]

Orpah, too, did not escape the rabbis' censure. Her
name, for example, was understood to mean "nape of the
neck," because she turned her back upon her mother-in-
law.[28] Modern critics characterize her actions as an obedient response to Naomi's request, but the rabbis were
more critical of her decision. What happened to Orpah
after she returned home, they wondered. According to
Rabbi Judah, the four warriors mentioned in 2 Samuel
21:22 were Orpah's children, her reward for having traveled four miles with Naomi.[29] In the same verse, however,
we learn that these four warriors were killed by David, a
descendant of Ruth, and his men. Rabbi Berekiah insisted that as a reward for having gone forty paces with
Naomi, Orpah's son—who was none other than the
mighty Goliath—escaped punishment for forty days (see
1 Sam. 17:16).[30] But we know the fate that eventually
befell Goliath.[31] Moreover, Ruth Rabbah records the lamentable opinion that on the day she left her mother-in-
law, she was the victim of gang-rape.[32]

Naturally, Ruth's famous speech to her mother-in-law
caught the rabbis' attention as well. They believed that
after Orpah's departure, Ruth expressed her desire to
convert to Judaism. Naomi first fulfilled her responsibility thrice to dissuade the would-be convert (Ruth 1:8, 11,
12).[33] Finally, however, she told her what conversion
would entail. Her instructions, of course, are not recorded in the biblical text. Ruth's responses to Naomi do
appear, however. The rabbis' job, therefore, was to recover Naomi's words—uttered, as it were, "between the
lines of the text."[34] So, for example, when Naomi advised, "It is not the custom of the daughters of Israel to

frequent Gentile theatres and circuses," Ruth promised, "Where you go, I will go." When Naomi said, "We are forbidden seclusion between man and woman." Ruth responded, "Where you lodge, I will lodge." When Naomi warned, "We are forbidden idolatry," Ruth responded, "Your God is my God."[35]

Finally, the rabbis wondered why all the townsfolk were gathered in the square on the day of Naomi and Ruth's arrival in Bethlehem, so that a great crowd gathered around them. One astonishing explanation was that Naomi and Ruth arrived on the day of the funeral of Boaz's first wife.[36]

Scene Two

Like the end of Scene One (Ruth 1:22), Ruth 2:1 hints that the plight of "empty" Naomi may not be so desperate as it seems: "Now Naomi had a kinsman on her husband's side," we read, "a man of substance, of the family of Elimelech, whose name was Boaz." When Ruth sets out to glean and, "as luck would have it" (2:3), winds up in Boaz's field, we suspect that more than mere luck is at work here.[37]

Diligent in her labor, Ruth unwittingly attracts the attention of both the overseer and his master, who has just arrived on the scene.[38] The rabbis explained why Ruth caught their eyes:

> All the other women bend down to gather the ears of corn, but she sits and gathers; all the other women hitch up their skirts, and she keeps hers down; all the other women jest with the reapers, while she is reserved; all the other women gather from between the sheaves, while she gathers from that which is already abandoned.[39]

Learning of Ruth's relationship to Naomi, Boaz ensures her safety throughout the remainder of the grain harvest (2:8–9) and even authorizes what one commentator has called "a little generous cheating on her behalf (v. 15)."[40] Moreover, he blesses Ruth for her faithfulness to her mother-in-law, saying "May the Lord reward your deeds. May you have a full recompense from the Lord, the God of Israel, under whose wings you have sought refuge" (2:12).[41] That evening, when Naomi realizes that Ruth has gleaned in the field of her kinsman, she blesses Boaz in the name of YHWH, "whose kindness has not forsaken the living or the dead" (2:20b, RSV).

Scene Three

Determined to relieve the barrenness of both her family line and Ruth, Naomi devises a plan. She instructs her daughter-in-law to "bathe, anoint yourself, dress up, and go down to the threshing floor" (Ruth 3:3) where Boaz will pass the night. Having located him there, Ruth is to "go over and uncover his feet and lie down" (3:4).

Why, you may wonder, was Boaz sleeping at the threshing floor?[42] The rabbis offered at least two explanations. The great eleventh-century rabbi, Rashi, believed that Boaz's generation was so sinful (witness the violent upheavals described in the book of Judges) that he was forced to sleep there to protect his grain from robbers. Another view, however, was based upon Hosea 9:1c: "You have loved a harlot's fee by every threshing floor of new grain." Obviously, some rabbis concluded, Boaz slept there in order to ensure that *his* threshing floor was not used for unchaste purposes.[43]

Ruth obeys Naomi, her preparations resembling those of a bride for her groom. In a scene replete with sexual nuances, she goes to Boaz. The Bible describes their encounter:

> [6]So she went down to the threshing floor and did just as her mother-in-law had told her. [7]And when

Boaz had eaten and drunk, and his heart was merry, he
went to lie down at the end of the heap of grain. Then
she came softly and uncovered his feet, and lay down.
[8]At midnight the man was startled, and turned over,
and behold, a woman lay at his feet! [9]He said, "Who
are you?" And she answered, "I am Ruth, your
maidservant; spread your skirt over your maidservant,
for you are next of kin." (Ruth 3:6–9, RSV)[44]

If you know Hebrew, you recognize that the very
meaning "to lie down" refers to sexual intercourse in
some contexts.[45] The Hebrew word for "feet" may be
used euphemistically to refer to genitals.[46] Furthermore,
Ruth's request that Boaz "spread your skirt over your
maidservant," echoes metaphorical descriptions of betrothal (cf. Ezek. 16:8). The scene is certainly suggestive.
Did Boaz and Ruth engage in sexual intercourse that
night? As we shall see, the rabbis went to great effort to
show that they did not. Quite apart from their opinion,
however, an argument for sexual consummation on that
occasion goes beyond what the text states and runs
counter to the characterization of Ruth and Boaz as persons of unblemished virtue.[47]

Rabbinical Interpretations of the Encounter at the Threshing Floor

According to the Talmud, a man may betroth himself
to a woman in one of three ways: (1) by giving her an
object greater than one cent in value and making a declaration of betrothal; (2) by document; and (3) through
sexual intercourse.[48] In their discussions of the scene at
the threshing floor, however, the commentators made it
clear that Boaz did not exercise the third option.

According to Ruth Rabbah, Boaz was "in a cheerful
mood" (Ruth 3:7) when he went to bed because "he re-

cited the grace after meals," "he ate different kinds of
sweet things after his meal, as they accustom the tongue
to the Torah," and "he occupied himself with the words
of the Torah . . . " (Ruth Rabbah V. 15, p. 71). Moreover, he was seeking a wife; and, as Proverbs 18:22
teaches us, "*Whosoever findeth a wife findeth a good thing*"
(Ruth Rabbah V 15, p. 71). The Targum (iii 8)[49]adds that
when Boaz awoke to discover a woman at his feet, " 'he
restrained his desire and did not go near her, even as did
Joseph the Righteous, who refused to go near the Egyptian woman, his master's wife,[50] and even as did Paltiel
the Pious, the son of Laish, who placed a sword between
himself and Michal daughter of Saul, David's wife, and
refused to go near her'."[51] "R. Judah said: "All that night
his Evil Inclination contended with him, saying, 'You are
unmarried and seek a wife, and she is unmarried and
seeks a husband. Arise and have intercourse with her,
and make her your wife.' And he took an oath to his Evil
Inclination, saying, 'As the Lord liveth, I will not touch
her.' "[52]

In addition to establishing Boaz's moral resolve, the
rabbis were interested in illumining certain details of this
late-night encounter. According to Ruth Rabbah, for example, the beginning of the conversation between Ruth
and Boaz was longer than the few words recorded in
verse 9. When Boaz first discovered Ruth, he feared that
she might be a spirit. Touching her hair, however, he
realized that she must be mortal, because "spirits have no
hair." He therefore said,

> "WHO ART THOU? (*ib.* 9), a woman or a spirit?" She
> answered, "A woman." "A maiden or a married
> woman?" She answered, "A maiden." "Art thou clean
> or unclean?" She answered, "Clean." AND BEHOLD
> A WOMAN, purest of women, LAY AT HIS FEET (*ib.*
> 8), as it is said, AND HE SAID: WHO ART THOU?
> AND SHE ANSWERED: I AM RUTH THY
> HANDMAID."[53]

Levirate Marriage

Although the events that transpired on the threshing floor remain a mystery, despite the best efforts of the rabbis, scholars agree that Ruth's words, "Spread your skirt over your maidservant, for you are next of kin," expressed her hope that Boaz would enter into a levirate marriage with her—that is, a conjugal union that might produce an heir to preserve the patrilineage of her deceased husband, Mahlon.[54] (Hebrew law sanctioned the practice whereby a widow became the wife of her husband's brother, or other close relative, in order to have a child who would inherit her first husband's estate and preserve his name for the future.) Boaz responds favorably to Ruth's request, but he also acknowledges that there is a nearer kinsman whose right to Ruth precedes his own.

In the early hours of the morning, Ruth slips from the threshing floor.[55] Before she leaves, however, Boaz gives her grain, in order that she not go back to her mother-in-law "empty-handed."[56] Returning home, Ruth tells Naomi everything that has happened;[57] and Naomi, confident of Boaz's resolve, encourages Ruth, saying "Stay here, daughter. . . . For the man will not rest, but will settle the matter today" (Ruth 3:18).

Scene Four

True to Naomi's word, Boaz goes to the city gate, the traditional place for legal and business transactions. "Just then," the text states, the nearer redeemer happens along. The rabbis, of course, noticed this striking "coincidence," and Rav Shmuel bar Nachman observed that, "Had [the nearer kinsman] been at the opposite end of the earth God would have caused him to fly, so to speak, to be there, in order to relieve the righteous Boaz of the anxiety of waiting. . . . "[58] Calling the unnamed man aside,[59] Boaz gathers together the ten elders required to witness a legal transaction. When all the men are seated, Boaz speaks:

> [3]Naomi, now returned from the country of Moab, must sell the piece of land which belonged to our kinsman Elimelech. [4]I thought I should disclose the matter to you and say: Acquire it in the presence of those seated here and in the presence of the elders of my people. If you are willing to redeem it, redeem! But if you will not redeem, tell me, that I may know. For there is no one to redeem but you, and I come after you (Ruth 4:3–4a).

The nearer kinsman's response is immediate and affirmative: "I will redeem it," he says in verse 4b. Boaz speaks again, however, this time inserting both Ruth and a possible heir for Mahlon into the transaction: "The day you buy the field from the hand of Naomi, you are also buying[60] Ruth the Moabitess, the widow of the dead, in order to restore the name of the dead to his inheritance" (4:5, RSV).[61]

Now, the kinsman thinks twice and says: "Then I cannot redeem it for myself, lest I impair my own inheritance. You take over my right of redemption, for I am unable to exercise it" (v. 6).

What follows is a solemn, and to our minds strange, legal ritual. The kinsman takes off his sandal, gives it to Boaz, and says, "Acquire for yourself."[62] Boaz then addresses their audience, saying:

> [9]You are witnesses today that I am acquiring from Naomi all that belonged to Elimelech and all that belonged to Chilion and Mahlon. [10]I am also acquiring Ruth the Moabite, the wife of Mahlon, as my wife, so as to perpetuate the name of the deceased upon his estate, that the name of the deceased may not disappear from

among his kinsmen and from the gate of his home town. You are witnesses today (Ruth 4:9b–10).

Modern critics concede that Scene Four is confusing at a number of points. First, we are surprised to learn that Naomi owns a plot of land. The property is nowhere mentioned prior to this point, and the reference to it here raises some serious questions. If, for example, Naomi was a landowner, why was Ruth reduced to gleaning for their food?[63] Was male assistance required by women seeking to reclaim family land after a prolonged absence from it (a possibility suggested by 2 Kings 8:1–6)? Again, why are purchasing the land and marrying Ruth linked? The book of Ruth seems to presuppose that the duties of levirate marriage and land redemption (i.e., assuming responsibility for both the land and the dependents of its former owner) go hand in hand, but biblical scholars remind us that no extant law code within the Hebrew Bible pairs them. Moreover, it seems unlikely that her closest living family member would have known nothing of Naomi's return to Bethlehem prior to his conversation with Boaz at the town gate. We raise these issues, but we cannot resolve them. Greater knowledge of ancient Israelite laws and social practices might resolve a few difficulties, but it is also likely that the storyteller exercised some artistic freedom in order to construct a satisfying plot.

Scene Four ends as the elders, along with others at the gate, accept their role as witnesses and recite a marriage blessing that, although addressed to Boaz, has as its object his bride and, more specifically, her future fertility:

[11]May Yahweh make the woman who is joining your
    family
  like Rachel and like Leah
  who together built up the family of Israel,
So that you may produce abundant progeny in
    Ephrathah
  and leave a big family name in Bethlehem

> [12]And so that your family
>   may be like the family of Perez
>   whom Tamar bore to Judah
>   through the offspring Yahweh may grant you
>   through this maid (Ruth 4:11b–12, Parker).[64]

Ruth was compared to Leah and Rachel, the rabbis said, because like them she was a foreign woman who left nonrighteous parents "to cleave to God and a righteous husband."[65]

Scene Five

> So Boaz married Ruth; she became his wife, and he cohabited with her. The Lord gave her a conception, and she bore a son (Ruth 4:13).[66]

How great is the contrast between this union and Ruth's ten barren years of marriage to Mahlon! The birth of tiny Obed unites the townswomen in praise to YHWH, who "has not withheld a redeemer from you [Naomi] today!" (4:14). Ruth, too, is singled out for extraordinary praise: She is more to Naomi than seven sons—and in our Hebrew scriptures, it doesn't get any better than that![67] Naomi's earlier complaint, "I went away full, and the Lord has brought me back empty" (1:21), is addressed, in part at least. Naomi is comforted by the baby and by her daughter-in-law's love (4:15). However, one child can never be replaced by another. Unlike the rabbis, the biblical author offers no explanation for the tragic loss of Naomi's own husband and sons.[68]

According to a Midrash attributed to Yalkut Shimoni,[69] Boaz perished after only one day of marriage to Ruth.[70] His death was interpreted by some as punishment for marrying a foreigner. Only in later years, when the families of Obed and his son, Jesse, prospered, did the Israelites come to recognize that God had truly blessed their union and that the law, "No Ammonite or Moabite shall be admitted into the congregation of the Lord" (Deut. 23:4),[71] referred to foreign men only, since scripture did not say, "No Ammonitess or Moabitess shall enter. . . ."[72]

Date of Composition

The Babylonian Talmud identifies Samuel as the author of Judges and Ruth as well as the book (1–2 Samuel, originally one scroll) that bears his name.[73] Most contemporary commentators, however, believe that in its final form Ruth derives from a post-exilic author—that is, an individual living in Palestine some years after Cyrus' liberating edict (about 538 B.C.E.) gave the exiled Judeans permission to leave Babylon and return home.[74] Other biblical writings from this period also reflect the struggles of a Jewish community wrestling with questions of inclusiveness. In Ezra 10:1–44, for example, we read the heartbreaking account of families torn apart when Jewish men were required to expel their foreign wives as well as the children born of such unions. Ruth speaks to such a social crisis in a powerful, albeit nonaggressive manner, for the book gently affirms that no less an individual than King David himself counted among his forebears a righteous Moabitess.[75]

Ruth: Jewish Convert
Par Excellence

What, then, was the rabbis' view of Ruth the Moabitess? She was, to their minds, the paradigmatic convert to Judaism. A princess in her own land, she turned her back upon wicked Moab and its worthless idols to become a God-fearing Jewess—loyal daughter-in-law, modest bride, renowned ancestress of Israel's great King David. The *Iggeres Shmuel* goes so far as to express the astonishing opinion that Ruth's merit exceeded that of Abraham, Israel's first patriarch, since he left home only after God commanded him to (Gen. 12:1), while Ruth "left on her own initiative—without a divine call, and despite the dissuasion of her mother-in-law—in order to come under the wings" of God.[76]

Feminist Interpretations of Ruth

The rabbis' esteemed view of Ruth is shared by millions of modern women and men who recognize her strength of character and admire her quiet courage. We may, using contemporary labels, call the book a "love story"; and it is true that Ruth's beautiful and moving speech to Naomi has been recited by countless brides to their grooms during nuptials. If Ruth be a love story, however, it is a story of the familial love that binds two women (Ruth 1:16–17; 4:15b).[77]

Given the book's popularity, it is perhaps surprising to discover that contemporary feminist scholars give Ruth mixed reviews. While not a few women find much in the book that is praiseworthy, others question an uncritical willingness to fall in with the role model presented by the biblical narrator, attractively packaged though it is in the person of Ruth.

Perhaps the most eloquent spokesperson for the first of these two positions is Phyllis Trible. In a sensitive and insightful study, Trible emphasizes Naomi and Ruth's independence, intelligence, and commitment.[78] To be sure, she recognizes that the patriarchal nature of ancient Israelite society has left its prints upon the scroll. Patriarchy obtrudes, for example, in Boaz's question to his overseer ("Whose girl is that?" [2:5]), which presupposes that women are both the property, and the responsibility, of men—first their fathers, and then their husbands. It also permeates the scene at the town gate, where male perspectives and concerns predominate and men determine women's fates. As Trible points out (and the overseer's response implicitly acknowledges [2:6]), however, Ruth cannot be defined according to traditional categories. She belongs to no man, and she (with Naomi) takes the initiative to determine her own destiny. Moreover, the patriarchal cast of the encounter between Boaz and the nearer kinsman is balanced in the following scene, Trible argues, by the words and actions of the townswomen who gather around Naomi and her grandchild:

> Their language of naming returns to the theme that Boaz introduced and the elders reinforced: "to restore the name of the dead to his inheritance." By concentrating upon it, the men shifted emphasis from justice for living females to justice for dead males. This shift was jarring in a story of women, even if it was justified in a world of men, but now the women redeem this male theme. They identify the child as the son of Naomi rather than of Elimelech. They perceive this infant as restoring life to the living rather than restoring a name to the dead. They speak of Ruth the bearer rather than of Boaz the begetter. And they themselves name the baby.[79]

Trible believes, therefore, that women can find much to celebrate and emulate in the book of Ruth. Naomi and her daughter-in-law don't just survive their difficult circumstances; they challenge and seek to transform their culture.[80] "With consummate artistry," Trible writes,

the book of Ruth presents the aged Naomi and the
youthful Ruth as they struggle for survival in a patriarchal environment. These women bear their own bur-
dens. They know hardship, danger, insecurity and
death. No God promises them blessing; no man rushes
to their rescue. They themselves risk bold decisions
and shocking acts to work out their own salvation in
the midst of the alien, the hostile, and the unknown.[81]

Other scholars believe, however, that Ruth, the character, is a role model whose ostensible motivations and actions must be thoughtfully scrutinized, since they actually
reflect the concerns and values of the anonymous biblical
narrator. In chapter 1, we noted some feminists' intense
interest in uncovering the presuppositions, convictions,
and literary strategies of biblical authors, most of whom
never stepped forward to tell why, when, where, or
precisely for whom they wrote.[82] The narrator of Ruth
implicitly purports simply to relate events "as they happened," in a straightforward and reliable fashion. As
readers, we scarcely are aware of his presence, except
when he pauses to provide us with some background information about an obscure legal ritual (4:7). We do well,
however, to remember that this sense of objectivity is an
illusion, the result of a skillful author's efforts.[83] The
book of Ruth is not a window allowing us to see back into
the past clearly and without distortion. It is, rather, a
canvas upon which every brush stroke has been placed
deliberately and with great care. Some brush strokes may
create images that approximate real objects and events.
Others may introduce features that existed only in the
mind of the artist. Always, however, the artist (author)
controls the composition—and to no small extent our
comprehension of it as well.[84]

What are some of the values and concerns that motivated the narrator of Ruth's story to speak or write as he
did? For Esther Fuchs, careful reading reveals that the
biblical narrator has projected onto Ruth the desires that

he most values and that he most wishes women to embrace as well. In a provocative article entitled, "The Literary Characterization of Mothers and Sexual Politics in the Hebrew Bible," Fuchs writes:

> Ruth . . . is extolled as a heroine, thanks to her faithfulness to her deceased husband's patrilineage. What turns her into a biblical heroine is not the fact that she prefers to follow Naomi to the land of Judah rather than to stay in Moab, but the fact that Naomi is her mother-in-law, the mother of Mahlon, her deceased husband who left her childless. She is not merely extolled for her ability to survive physically in adverse circumstances or for her initiative and energy in general, as some would have it, but for her success in finding and marrying a direct relative of Elimelech, her father-in-law, and giving birth to children who would carry on the patrilineage of her deceased husband.[85]

Baby boy Obed is conspicuously in view when Ruth is praised by the townswomen as "more than seven sons" to Naomi (4:15b), and when her mother-in-law's life is "renewed" (4:15a). These two women are prized and fulfilled because they have successfully implemented a strategy leading to the birth of this male child, thereby ensuring that "the name of the deceased may not disappear from among his kinsmen and from the gate of his home town."[86]

Fuchs notes, however, that "the biblical narrative is careful *not* to establish too close a link between the interests of patriarchy and woman's sacrifice. On the contrary, the heroine's motivation is normally shown to be self-seeking."[87] In other words, what men most want from women, the biblical authors depict as what women most want for themselves.[88] Ruth, for example, is depicted as wanting to leave behind her gods, family and friends, and homeland, in order to accompany her mother-in-law to a foreign land where she will live among strangers.[89] "By projecting onto woman what man desires most," Fuchs observes, "the biblical narrative creates a powerful role model for women . . . [and] it should be ascribed to the imaginative and artistic ingenuity of the biblical narrator that one of the most vital patriarchal concerns [continuing the male line] is repeatedly presented not as an imposition on women but as something she herself desires more than anything else."[90]

Conclusion

Who is Ruth? A paradigm of faithfulness, a puppet in the service of patriarchy, or a radical call to inclusiveness? She is, I suspect, something of each—more complex than we initially think, because those who spoke and wrote about her were not themselves one-dimensional, and because the act of reading draws Ruth into our own complex interpretive webs as well. In this chapter, we have encountered the questions of biblical scholars, been enriched by the contributions of the rabbis, and pondered conflicting interpretations advanced by contemporary feminists. But what will be your answer to the question "Who is Ruth?"

Notes

1. Ruth Rabbah II 14, p. 35. The abbreviation "R." stands for "rabbi."

2. James Barr notes the fallacy of using this phrase to denote the ancient times about which the Hebrew Bible speaks. For most of the period covered in the Old Testament, Israel had no scripture in the sense of a delimited, authoritative collection of religious texts. Since the emergence of a Hebrew Bible post-dates most of ancient Israel's history, we, more than Miriam or Ruth, are living in "biblical times" (i.e., times when there is a Bible). See *Holy Scripture: Canon, Authority, Criticism,* pp. 1–2.

3. Moab was a small state lying east of the Dead Sea. See *The Interpreter's Dictionary of the Bible,* s.v. "Moab."

4. Num. 22:1–6. The kingdom of Moab lay just east of the Dead Sea.

5. The Arnon (modern Wadi Mojib) is a stream that flows from the Transjordan plateau through a steep canyon into the Dead Sea. *The Interpreter's Dictionary of the Bible,* s.v. "Arnon."

6. Jer. 48:16, 20.

7. Isa. 25:10 (RSV).

8. Deut. 23:4.

9. In ancient Israel, barrenness was construed as an act of God, divine punishment, or, at least, an indication of divine disapproval (Gen. 20:18; 1 Sam. 1:5–6; 2 Sam. 6:16–23; Hos. 9:14–16). See Bird's informative article, "Images of Women in the Old Testament," pp. 41–88, especially pp. 60–63.

10. This statement holds true for both Jews and Protestant Christians. Roman Catholic and Orthodox Christians add the deuterocanonical book of Judith to their list of biblical books named for women.

11. The term "levirate" comes from the word "levir," mean-

ing "a husband's brother." As we shall see, levirate marriage refers to the union of a widow and her deceased husband's brother (or another close relative if her husband had no brothers, or if they predeceased him).

12. The generic designation, "Writings," reflects the tremendous diversity of literary types included in this part of the canon.

13. In Jewish tradition, Ruth is one of the *Megilloth,* the five scrolls (Song of Songs, Ruth, Lamentations, Ecclesiastes, and Esther) read at various festivals during the liturgical year. *Tanakh* follows Jewish practice in grouping these five scrolls and placing them after the book of Job.

14. The period of the judges began with the establishment of Israel in Canaan (about 1200 B.C.E.) and ended with the institution of the monarchy (about 1020 B.C.E.).

15. See Phyllis Trible's insightful and moving study, "An Unnamed Woman: The Extravagance of Violence," in *Texts of Terror,* pp. 65–91.

16. *Tanakh* identifies this phrase as a formula of imprecation. The word "thus" suggests that Ruth's words were accompanied by some gesture.

17. "pleasant one"

18. "bitter one"

19. "Shaddai" is a biblical name for God, using here as a synonym for Yahweh. According to the priestly tradition, God was worshiped under the name El Shaddai during the period of the matriarchs and patriarchs (Exod. 6:2–3). In a very technical discussion, Cross argues that the original meaning of Shaddai was "breast" (*Canaanite Myth and Hebrew Epic,* pp. 52–60). Trible notes a wordplay in Gen. 49:25, where the "God of your father" is paralleled by "Shaddai," "the God of the breasts [who] gives the blessings of the breasts" (*Interpreter's Dictionary of the Bible Supplement,* s.v. "God, Nature of, in the OT").

20. Among the rabbinical interpretations of these words, we find the opinion that Naomi was pregnant when she and her family migrated to Moab (Ruth Rabbah III 7, p. 48).

21. Green explores the "seed restoration" theme in the book of Ruth in "The Plot of the Biblical Story of Ruth," pp. 55–68; see also Rauber, "Literary Values in the Bible: The Book of Ruth," pp. 27–37.

22. This manuscript was virtually completed when I enjoyed

the opportunity to hear a lecture by Elie Wiesel, Nobel Laureate for Peace and Andrew W. Mellon Professor at Boston University, entitled "In the Bible: Ruth or Welcoming Strangers." Although 1:20 testifies to Naomi's ability to speak her mind, Wiesel noted her unobtrusive personality, her tendency to keep quiet and conceal her feelings, thereby avoiding controversy; Naomi did not, for example, rebuke her sons when they married Moabite women. In fact, Wiesel suggested, the book of Ruth should really have been named after Naomi, but she vetoed the idea!

23. Between the initial, brief notice of loss of family and the final restoration of family at the story's end, the plot develops according to the special interests of the narrator. See Parker, *The Pre-Biblical Narrative Tradition*, pp. 164–165.

24. For these and additional views, see *The Book of Ruth/ Megillas Ruth*, Scherman and Zlotowitz, eds., pp. 61–63. The ArtScroll Tanach Series is an invaluable, albeit extremely conservative, resource for readers desiring access to insights from selected rabbinical interpreters—ancient, medieval, and modern.

25. Ibid., pp. 62–63.

26. According to Rabbi Meir, "they neither proselytised [their wives], nor gave them ritual immersion," i.e., they did not cause them to convert to Judaism (Ruth Rabbah II 9, p. 30); see also Beattie, *Jewish Exegesis of the Book of Ruth*, p. 171, where the words of the Targumist are quoted: "They transgressed against the decree of the word of the Lord and they took for themselves foreign wives from the daughters of Moab . . . and because they transgressed against the decree of the word of the Lord and contracted affinity with foreign peoples their days were cut off and both Mahlon and Chilion also died in the polluted land."

27. *The Book of Ruth/Megillas Ruth*, p. 67.

28. Ruth Rabbah II 9, p. 31.

29. Another opinion held that the warriors were her reward for having shed four tears for her mother-in-law (twice she wept [Ruth 1:9, 14], using both eyes; hence, four tears). See Beattie, *Jewish Exegesis*, p. 192.

30. Ruth Rabbah II 20, p. 38.

31. According to 2 Sam. 21:19, Goliath was one of the four warriors killed by David's men. Verse 19 states that "Elhanan, son of Jaare-oregim the Bethlehemite, killed Goliath the Git-

tite." Tradition, of course, identified David as the slayer of Goliath (1 Sam. 17:45–51). The text in 2 Samuel may, however, preserve an older tradition. The Chronicler seeks to reconcile the two stories in Samuel by stating that Elhanan actually killed Goliath's brother, and not Goliath himself (1 Chron. 20:5).

32. According to Ruth Rabbah II 20, p. 39, "a hundred heathens raped her."

33. *The Book of Ruth/Megillas Ruth,* p. 72.

34. Beattie, *Jewish Exegesis,* p. 173.

35. Ibid., pp. 173–174; Ruth Rabbah II 22–24, pp. 39–40.

36. Ruth Rabbah III 6 attributes to Rabbi Joshua ben Abin these words: "It is written, *O Lord God of Hosts, who is a mighty one, like unto Thee, O Lord* (Ps. LXXXIX, 9), who brings things about in their due season. The wife of Boaz died on that day, and all Israel assembled to pay their respects, and just then Ruth entered with Naomi. Thus one was taken out when the other entered. . . . " (p. 47).

37. Israelite law stipulated that the needy be permitted to glean (that is, to gather) loose stalks of grain left behind by the reapers (Lev. 19:9–10, 23:22; Deut. 24:19).

38. The biblical reference to a single overseer provided the rabbis with both a question, "How many servants were working in Boaz's field?" and its answer, "forty-two." How did they arrive at this number? Because Boaz had only one overseer, while Solomon appointed 3,600 overseers over 150,000 workers (2 Chron. 2:17). 150,000 divided by 3,600 equals approximately forty-two. It's a simple matter of division! (Ruth Rabbah IV 6, p. 55).

39. Ruth Rabbah IV 5, p. 55.

40. Robert C. Dentan, ed., *The Oxford Annotated Bible* (New York: Oxford University Press, 1962), p. 326.

41. When Boaz referred to Ruth leaving behind her "father and mother," he was, the rabbis claimed (Ruth Rabbah V 3, p. 60), commending her for rejecting idolatry. See Jer. 2:27: "They said to wood, 'You are my father,' to stone, 'You gave birth to me.' "

42. Quoted in Beattie, *Jewish Exegesis,* p. 103.

43. Ruth Rabbah V 15, p. 72.

44. Although Naomi, in her instructions to Ruth, said that Boaz would tell her what to do (3:4b), Ruth actually tells Boaz what to do.

45. *skb*; see, for example, Gen. 19:33, 35; Ezek. 23:8 (metaphorical); Micah 7:5.

46. Isa. 7:20.

47. See, for example, 3:14.

48. *Kiddushin 2a*; see Hauptman, "Images of Women in the Talmud," p. 185.

49. Targums are Aramaic translations of Hebrew texts. They were written to assist Aramaic-speaking Jews who could not easily understand biblical texts read in the original Hebrew. These "translations" often included interpretive and homiletical additions as well.

50. Gen. 39:7–10.

51. These quotations from the Targum, as well as an explanation of the rabbi's reference to Palti[el] (see 1 Sam. 25:44 and 2 Sam. 3:15–16), appear in Beattie, *Jewish Exegesis*, p. 179.

52. Ruth Rabbah VI 4, p. 81.

53. Ruth Rabbah VI 1, pp. 74–75. In *Midrash Rabbah*, the text under analysis appears in capital letters. Commentary appears in normal type, while citations of additional scriptural passages appear in italics.

54. See also Gen. 38:6–26, Deut. 25:5–10, and the section on "The levirate" in *The Interpreter's Dictionary of the Bible Supplement*, s.v. "Marriage."

55. According to Ruth Rabbah VII 1, p. 82, "R. Hunya and R. Jeremiah in the name of R. Samuel b. R. Isaac said: All that night Boaz lay stretched out upon his face, and prayed, 'Lord of the Universe, it is revealed and known to Thee that I did not touch her; so may it be Thy will that it be not known that the woman came to the threshing-floor, that the name of Heaven be not profaned through me.' " *The Book of Ruth/Megillas Ruth* quotes from Alshich, a sixteenth-century commentator who held that when Boaz prayed that Ruth not be discovered, "he wasn't concerned for his own reputation; he was known as . . . *a righteous man*, and he was old—he would not be accused of unbecoming conduct. It was Ruth's reputation he was concerned with; after all *she* went out in the middle of the night! He therefore specified *that it not be known that* the woman *came to the threshing-floor*" (p. 117).

56. Exactly how much grain Ruth received from Boaz is not clear, for the text simply says that he gave her "six barleys." Commentators have proposed a variety of solutions. See the

discussion in Campbell, *Ruth,* pp. 127–128. In the Talmud we read that "he symbolically alluded to her [by giving her a token six barley grains] that six righteous men, each possessing six outstanding virtues, are destined to descend from this marriage: David, the Messiah, Daniel, Hananiah, Mishael and Azariah" (*Sanhedrin 93a–b,* quoted in *The Book of Ruth/Megillas Ruth,* p. 118).

57. According to the Hebrew text, when Ruth saw Naomi, her mother-in-law asked, "Who are you, my daughter?" Translators appropriately render the question as "How is it with you, daughter?" (*Tanakh*), or the like. Ruth Rabbah (VII 4, p.84) suggests, however, that behind Naomi's "Who are you, my daughter?" was another question: "Are you still a virgin [maiden] or a married women?"

58. Quoted in *The Book of Ruth/Megillas Ruth,* p. 120.

59. According to 4:1, Boaz says, "Come over and sit down here, So-and-so." The Hebrew text refers to the nearer kinsman as *pĕlōnî 'almōnî,* two rhyming nouns that are not proper names, but rather designate one whose actual name will not be given. In *Ruth,* Campbell tentatively suggests that the phrase may originally have contributed a sense of privacy to Boaz's initial words (pp. 141–143).

60. Building upon Weiss' study of Mishnaic uses of the verb *qnh* ("to buy") for marriage, Campbell suggests that in 4:5 the text speaks of "buying" Ruth because the marriage is related to a larger commercial transaction, the purchase of Elimelech's portion of the village's cultivated land (*Ruth,* pp. 146–147).

61. *The Book of Ruth/Megillas Ruth* records Rav Shmuel de Uzeda's view (in *Iggeres Shmuel,* a commentary he published in the sixteenth century) that Boaz stressed Ruth's country of origin and the memory of her now deceased husband, in order to discourage the nearer kinsman from the act of redemption (p. 124).

62. So most commentators. Campbell, however, leaves open the possibility that the ritual entailed an exchange of sandals between both parties (*Ruth,* pp. 149–150).

63. Malbim (Meir Leibush ben Yechiel Michel), a nineteenth-century commentator, resolved this difficulty by pointing to 1:22. Because Naomi and Ruth arrived in Bethlehem "at the beginning of the barley harvest," he explained, it was too late

to plant crops in the field belonging to Elimelech's family (*The Book of Ruth/Megillas Ruth*, p. 85).

64. This translation is by Simon B. Parker, whose book *The Pre-Biblical Narrative Tradition* includes a helpful discussion of biblical and extra-biblical marriage blessings in the ancient Near Eastern world (pp. 87–98).

65. *The Book of Ruth/Megillas Ruth*, pp. 130–131.

66. This translation is my own. Here is stated one facet of the ancient Israelite belief that God labors in the wombs of women, bringing about conception, fashioning the fetus, and strengthening women for labor and delivery (see also Gen. 30:2; 1 Sam. 1:19–20; Job 10:18, 31:13–15; Jer. 1:5; Isa. 66:9).

67. See Parker, *Pre-Biblical Narrative Tradition*, pp. 89–90.

68. But see above, n. 22.

69. Shimoni, the thirteenth-century author of an extensive midrashic anthology, is cited in *The Book of Ruth/Megillas Ruth*, p. 131.

70. See also Beattie, *Jewish Exegesis*, p. 194.

71. In English translations other than *Tanakh*, the reference is Deut. 23:3.

72. See Ruth Rabbah II 9, pp. 30–31.

73. *Baba Bathra 14b*.

74. In his commentary, Campbell dates Ruth much earlier, between 950 and 700 B.C.E., and most likely in the ninth century. See his discussion in *Ruth*, pp. 23–28.

75. According to 1 Sam. 22:3–5, David's parents went to Moab during his early "outlaw" period.

76. Quoted in *The Book of Ruth/Megillas Ruth*, p. 96.

77. Renita Weems emphasizes the friendship and devotion shared by Ruth and Naomi in "Blessed Be the Tie that Binds," in *Just A Sister Away*, pp. 23–36.

78. Trible, "A Human Comedy," in *God and the Rhetoric of Sexuality*, pp. 166–199.

79. Ibid., p. 194.

80. Ibid., p. 196.

81. Ibid., p. 166.

82. The book of Ruth nowhere claims that one of its characters, major or minor, composed the scroll. On the contrary, the entire story is anonymous third-person narrative.

83. See Booth, *The Rhetoric of Fiction*.

84. Of course, no author can control readers' responses completely. Narratives always contain gaps, which readers fill according to their own presuppositions, experience, knowledge, and point of view.

85. Fuchs, "Literary Characterizations of Mothers," p. 130. Fuchs defines "sexual politics" as "refer[ring] to the power-structured relations between men and women and, more specifically, to the economic, social, and ideological arrangements whereby males have traditionally controlled females." She refers readers to Millet, *Sexual Politics,* pp. 31–81.

86. 4:10. Of course, readers learn other lessons from Ruth as well, such as how foreigners should relate to Israelites and how young people should treat their elders. The text says nothing of Ruth's relationship with, or concern for, her countrywoman, peer, and sister-in-law, Orpah.

87. Fuchs, "Literary Characterization of Mothers," p. 130.

88. Fuchs recognizes, of course, that in ancient Israelite society women may well have conformed to patriarchal expectations and demands by choice, since conformity helped ensure survival, security, and social standing.

89. By the same token, the townswomen's remarks at the end of Scene Five that, for Trible, appear to "redeem this male theme" (*God and the Rhetoric of Sexuality*, p. 194), may rather be understood as the author's skillful means of modeling how women can claim, articulate, and support patriarchal concerns and institutions such as levirate marriage.

90. Fuchs, "Literary Characterization of Mothers," p. 130.

More than the Stars
of the Heavens:
Critical, Rabbinical,
and Feminist Perspectives
on Sarah

In 587 B.C.E., Babylonian soldiers breached the wall surrounding Jerusalem, ending a lengthy, crippling siege that had left the city's inhabitants starving. The king of Judah, Zedekiah, attempted to flee with some of his soldiers; but the Babylonians overtook them and brought the hapless monarch to Nebuchadrezzar, King of Babylon, who pronounced judgment upon him. Zedekiah's punishment was horrible, indeed. He was forced to witness the execution of his own sons; and then he was blinded and led away to Babylon in chains (2 Kings 25:1–7).

Meanwhile, the victorious troops burned every great building in Jerusalem, including the temple that Solomon

had built and dedicated to YHWH almost four hundred
years earlier. They captured many of the leaders within
Judean society—members of the royal administration,
priests, sages, craftsmen—and forced them to walk hun-
dreds of miles to Babylon to live as aliens in the midst of
their conquerors.

The Bible tells us precious little about what happened
to these exiles following their arrival in Babylon. However, texts like Psalm 137 testify to the pain and despair
they endured:

<blockquote>

[1]By the rivers of Babylon,
    there we sat,
    sat and wept,
    as we thought of Zion.
[2]There on the poplars
we hung up our lyres,
[3]for our captors asked us there for songs,
our tormentors, for amusement,
    "Sing us one of the songs of Zion."
[4]How can we sing a song of the Lord
    on alien soil?
[5]If I forget you, O Jerusalem,
    let my right hand wither;
[6]let my tongue stick to my palate
    if I cease to think of you,
    if I do not keep Jerusalem in memory
    even at my happiest hour.
[7]Remember, O Lord, against the Edomites
    the day of Jerusalem's fall;
    how they cried; "Strip her, strip her
    to her very foundations!"[1]
[8]Fair Babylon, you predator,
    a blessing on him who repays you in kind
    what you have inflicted on us;
    a blessing on him who seizes your babies
    and dashes them against the rocks! (Psalm 137:1–8).

</blockquote>

Modern readers undoubtedly wince at the severity of verses 7–8. We should not forget, however, the enormity of the exiles' losses. They were bereft of family members, friends, homes, and homeland—indeed, their very nation. Perhaps they had lost their God as well. Did not YHWH promise that a descendant of David would sit upon the throne in Jerusalem forever (2 Sam. 7:11b–16)? Now two Davidic kings, Jehoiachin and Zedekiah, were in Babylonian prisons; and the monarchy was no more.[2] Was not the Solomonic temple the place where YHWH's presence dwelt in a special way? Now the once glorious temple was a smoldering heap of rubble and ash. Was it not obvious that the God of Judah had been defeated by the superior power of the great Babylonian deity, Marduk?

Years and then decades passed. Despair collapsed into resignation and hopelessness. And then, deep in the heart of Babylon, deep in the midst of exile, an anonymous prophet evoked memory of a very old tradition, saying:

[1]Listen to Me, you who pursue justice,
You who seek the LORD;
Look to the rock you were hewn from,
To the quarry you were dug from.
[2]Look back to Abraham your father
and to Sarah who labored to bring you forth
(Isa. 51:1–2a).[3]

The prophet spoke to laughing young women and to heartbroken old men. He spoke to learned priests and sages and to the children who were playing on street corners. He spoke to mothers whose own mothers had been raped by the enemy troops that destroyed Jerusalem and to prosperous merchants who had done quite well for themselves in Babylon, thank you. He spoke to parents, to their children, and to their grandchildren, addressing those who remembered life in Jerusalem and those for whom Babylon was the only home they had ever known. He reminded them of an old, old story—the story of an elderly man and his childless wife, Sarah.

Who Was Sarah?

What was all this talk about rocks and quarry pits? About labor pains—women's work, and scarcely the topic of polite conversation! Who was Sarah, and what had an old lady's story to do with contemporary life in Babylon? Surely some of the exiles, at least, asked themselves these questions. Possibly they confronted this self-proclaimed prophet with them as well. Perhaps he had to remind his audience of their ancient tradition with words like these:

"Who was Sarah? Well, she was the wife of Abraham, of course. But we cannot define her simply by her relationship to a man. Like our great king, David, Sarah was a complex person—capable of great good, but also of grievous sin. She was a woman of courage. Along with her husband, she abandoned family, friends, homeland—all that was familiar, much that was beloved—in order to pursue a promise from God.

"As Abraham's wife, Sarah enjoyed privilege and power within her household. But despite her wealth and social standing, she was unhappy. You see, Sarah was barren—endlessly, hopelessly barren. God had closed her womb. Throughout the years of youth, and even middle age, Sarah hoped that YHWH would fulfill the promise that her descendants would be more numerous than the stars of the heaven. By the age of ninety, however, Sarah had faced the grief of barrenness. She was resigned to it. Her resignation was sometimes complacent, sometimes bitter. But either way, she was resigned. Sarah was without hope. She knew a hopeless situation when she saw one, *was* one. Her monthly periods had long since ceased. The pleasures of sex were, for Sarah, a thing of the past (Gen. 18:11–12).

"And so, when three strangers visited their tent, and one of them proclaimed that Sarah would bear a child in the spring—that she, like the land, would shake off the cold barren grip of winter, blossom and become fruitful, her dry body swelling up like a palm fruit, sweet as honey and flowing with milk—Sarah laughed (18:12). She chuckled at the impossibility of it all, snickered at the thought that her ninety-year-old womb could host a child. Sarah laughed, and that laughter was probably the only pleasure that barrenness had ever given her.

"But the stranger—was it indeed the Lord?—said to Abraham, "Why did Sarah laugh and say, 'Shall I in truth bear a child, old as I am?' Is anything too wondrous for the LORD? I will return to you at the time next year, and Sarah shall have a son" (18:13–14).

"And so it was. Sarah conceived and bore a child at the precise time foretold by God. Abraham named their baby boy Isaac, a name that means "he laughs." And Sarah's laughter, emitted once in disbelief, was returned to her not only in the form of laughing baby Isaac, but also in the good-natured laughter of everyone who heard about the wonderful thing that had happened to her."

Such was the story that the exilic prophet told to the Babylon-born children in his community who may never have heard it before. This was the story he brought to remembrance in the minds of those adults who had known such traditions once, long ago, but whose memory of them had faded over the years. "Look back to Abraham, your father, and to Sarah who brought you forth," he urged. As we shall see, at least some of the Babylonian exiles did look back, and, in their embrace of these and other of their ancient traditions, they discovered the courage to go back and begin a new life in Jerusalem.

Moreover, succeeding generations of Jews and Christians—men and women, rabbis, lay persons, biblical scholars, pastors, feminist and womanist interpreters—also have returned to the stories of Sarah and Abraham. Their discoveries are as diverse as the questions they bring to the text. Some commentators find in Sarah an unreasonable, oppressive woman; others perceive that she is herself oppressed. Some interpreters highlight her piety and religious gifts; others emphasize her embittered disbelief in the face of divine disclosure. A few scholars claim that we can learn nothing about her at all, so obfuscated is she by layers of reinterpretation and sexual stereotyping. For others, however, careful scrutiny of Sarah's story reveals traces of an ancient time when the biblical matriarchs played central, powerful roles in the religious and social lives of their communities.

The Abraham and Sarah Traditions

In our Bibles, the Abraham and Sarah traditions appear as a continuous narrative.[4] They begin when Terah, Abram's father, gathers his household and departs Ur of the Chaldeans for the land of Canaan (Gen. 11:31). They include stories of the couple's journeys and adventures, their encounters with the deity, their attempts to secure offspring, the birth and near sacrifice of Isaac, Sarah's death, Abraham's remarriage, and so on. Finally, they end with the death of Abraham and his burial in the cave of Machpelah (25:7–10).

Despite the traditions' unified appearance, however, many readers, ancient and modern, have questioned whether the Abraham and Sarah episodes were always the continuous narrative that we find in the book of Genesis. Consider, for example, the story of Hagar's expulsion from Abraham's household (21:9–21). Read alone, this tradition presupposes that Ishmael is a small child who, along with bread and a skin of water, can be carried upon his mother's back. Viewed within its broader narrative context, however, the Ishmael of this story must be at least fifteen years old.[5] Other episodes appear more than once in the Abraham and Sarah cycle, suggesting that they are variant forms of a single tradition. For example, the tale of the endangered matriarch occurs three times within the Pentateuch—twice concerning Sarah (12:10–20; 20:1–18), and once concerning Rebekah, the wife of Isaac (26:6–11).

Contemporary biblical scholars believe that the Abraham and Sarah cycle was not written during one period by a single author. On the contrary, traditions concerning the Hebrews' earliest ancestors, many of which began as oral traditions, circulated independently—the cherished memories of different groups that eventually united to form the biblical "people of Israel." At some point, probably early in the monarchical period of Israel's history (about 950 B.C.E.), an anonymous literary artist (the so-called "Yahwist") combined a number of those ancestral traditions, supplying linking passages and altering them where necessary in order to produce a coherent narrative. At a later time (probably after the destruction of Northern Israel by the Assyrians in 721 B.C.E.), this Yahwistic narrative was enriched by traditions from another literary source (composed by an author called "the Elohist").[6] Finally, another group of author-editors, the "Priestly writers," added additional materials and edited the entire work, producing the narrative in more or less its final form.[7] The creative effort of these editors was by no means a simple cut-and-paste operation. On the contrary, by their arrangement of and additions to traditions, they transformed the received materials such that originally discrete stories took their places within, and were informed by, the larger literary and theological agenda. For example, the motif of promise and fulfillment, so central to the Abraham and Sarah cycle, is not apparent in the single story of Pharaoh's decision to add Sarai to his harem (12:10–20). Read within its canonical context, however, the threat to Sarai imperils the fulfillment of God's promise that Abram and Sarai's offspring will inherit the land of Canaan, multiply greatly, and become a source of blessing to the nations.

A New Beginning

In the book of Genesis, the introduction of Abram and Sarai constitutes a new beginning, as it were, in the history of creation. To be sure, creation actually commences in Genesis 1 when God speaks light into existence, establishes a firmament in the midst of the waters, causes dry land to appear, brings about vegetation and various types of living creatures, and finally creates human beings, both male and female, "in the image of God" (Gen. 1:27). Genesis 2, originally an independent creation account, but in its present form and position intended to be read as a supplement to the preceding chapter, likewise describes the absolute origins of life, including human life. God's handiwork is "very good," and the first couple enjoys the blessings of life in the Garden of Eden.

But human beings prove unwilling to live in absolute obedience to their Creator (3:1–7). In the years following Adam and Eve's expulsion from Eden, their descendants multiply, but sinfulness thrives as well. YHWH therefore determines that a great flood will exterminate life on earth (save Noah, his family, and the animals taken aboard the ark) in order that creation can begin afresh. So fierce is the deluge that the earth almost returns to precreation chaos (7:11b); but at length the waters recede, and the ark's inhabitants repopulate the earth. Once more, however, human sinfulness (9:20–27), recalcitrance, and pride thwart the deity's intentions for creation. When humans resolve to build a great city with a towering ziggurat (step pyramid), God frustrates their ambition:

> [6]The LORD said, "If, as one people with one language for all, this is how they have begun to act, then nothing that they may propose to do will be out of their reach. [7]Let us,[8] then, go down and confound their speech there, so that they shall not understand one another's speech." [8]Thus the LORD scattered them from there over the face of the whole earth; and they stopped building the city. [9]That is why it was called Babel, because there the LORD confounded[9] the speech of the whole earth; and from there the LORD scattered them over the face of the whole earth (Gen. 11:6–9).

Tragically, the Babel episode ends with the people of the earth "dis-membered"—that is, scattered abroad and incapable of understanding one another.

In light of the preceding eleven chapters, then, the singling-out of Abram and Sarai appears as still another attempt by God to set things right, "to fashion an alternative community in creation gone awry, to embody in human history the power of the blessing":[10]

> [1]The Lord said to Abram, "Go forth from your native land and from your father's house to the land that I will show you.
> [2]I will make of you a great nation,
> And I will bless you;
> I will make your name great,
> And you shall be a blessing.
> [3]I will bless those who bless you
> And curse him that curses you;
> And all the families of the earth
> Shall bless themselves[11] by you" (Gen. 12:1–3).

This is a marvelous promise, to be sure. But how can it be fulfilled? In the preceding chapter (11:26–30), we learned that Sarai is barren. Infertility jeopardizes the divine pledge at its most basic level because, without progeny, the land cannot be retained beyond a single lifetime. A childless couple can scarcely become a great nation, and their influence upon "the families of the earth" will of necessity be short-lived. Barren Sarai is the potential undoing of the promise, the obstacle to its fulfillment.

The rabbis could not fail to notice that several of the matriarchs—Sarah, but also Rebekah and Rachael—endured years of barrenness before giving birth to sons, and they wondered why this was so. *Midrash Rabbah* records their various opinions, including the view that God withheld children from these women in order to ensure that their prayers not cease: "The Holy One, blessed be He, yearns for their prayers and supplications."[12] Another opinion held that the matriarchs, who were already beautiful and wealthy, might have become too independent had they been blessed also with sons while they were young. Yet another explanation, however, held that they were forced to endure barrenness in order that they might give the greatest possible pleasure to their husbands, since pregnant women are bloated and inelegant. Thus, the rabbis said, "The whole ninety years that Sarah did not bear she was like a bride in her canopy."[13]

Sarai Imperiled

In obedience to God's command, "Go forth from your native land," Abram assembles his household, including his wife Sarai and Lot, the son of his brother, and departs Haran for Canaan. Although the land already is inhabited (Gen. 12:6b), YHWH promises that it will belong to Abram's offspring. Abram builds an altar to the Lord in

Canaan—an auspicious occasion given the struggles between Yahwism and Canaanite religion that lie ahead for his distant descendants. When a severe famine strikes the land, however, Abram goes down to Egypt. Gerhard von Rad, a noted German biblical scholar and theologian, perceived in Abram's quick resort to Egypt an element of doubt concerning YHWH's ability to sustain both his family and the promise.[14] The rabbis saw it quite differently, however. They maintained that the famine, which occurred nowhere but in Canaan, was a test by God of Abram's faith. The patriarch endured this trial without voicing a single word of discontent or impatience; and since he was forced into Egypt for the sake of survival, he took advantage of the opportunity to acquire wisdom and to instruct Egypt's priests![15]

Just before Abram enters Egypt, he says to Sarai, "I know what a beautiful woman you are. If the Egyptians see you, and think, 'She is his wife,' they will kill me and let you live. Please say that you are my sister, that it may go well with me because of you, and that I may remain alive thanks to you" (12:11–13). One Jewish legend suggests that Abram did not actually know that his wife was beautiful until just a moment before he spoke, because—chaste man that he was—he had never before looked directly at her.[16] While they were crossing a stream, however, Abram inadvertently caught sight of her reflection in the water:

> Wherefore he spoke to her thus, "The Egyptians are very sensual, and I will put thee in a casket[17] that no harm befall me on account of thee." At the Egyptian boundary, the tax collectors asked him about the contents of the casket, and Abraham told them he had barley in it. "No," they said, "it contains wheat." "Very well," replied Abraham, "I am prepared to pay the tax on wheat." The officers then hazarded the guess, "It contains pepper!"[18] Abraham agreed to pay the tax on pepper, and when they charged him with

concealing gold in the casket, he did not refuse the pay the tax on gold, and finally on precious stones. Seeing that he demurred to no charge, however high, the tax collectors, made thoroughly suspicious, insisted upon his unfastening the casket and letting them examine the contents. When it was forced open, the whole of Egypt was resplendent with the beauty of Sarah. In comparison with her, all other beauties were like apes compared with men. She excelled Eve herself.[19]

The bedazzled Egyptian officials longed to possess her but recognized that such a prize should belong to no less than Pharaoh himself. And so they brought her to the royal palace, receiving for their efforts a handsome reward.[20]

The biblical text does not record Sarai's reaction to this sudden, dangerous turn of events. It simply notes that after she entered the harem, Abram's material holdings increased significantly: "And because of [Sarai], it went well with Abram; he acquired sheep, oxen, asses, male and female slaves, she-asses, and camels" (12:16). According to the rabbis, however, both Sarai and Abram were distraught; and each offered up piteous entreaties. A weeping Abraham prayed, "Is this the reward for my confidence in Thee? For the sake of Thy grace and Thy lovingkindness, let not my hope be put to shame." For her part, Sarai sought to remind the deity that Abram and she were not in such desperate straits by accident:

O God, Thou didst bid my lord Abraham leave his home, the land of his fathers, and journey to Canaan, and Thou didst promise him to do good unto him if he fulfilled Thy commands. And now we have done as Thou didst command us to do. We left our country and our kindred, and we journeyed to a strange land, unto a people which we knew not heretofore. We came hither to save our people from starvation, and now hath this terrible misfortune befallen. O Lord, help me and save me from the hand of this enemy, and for the sake of Thy grace show me good.[21]

According to the biblical text, YHWH does indeed rescue Sarai.[22] Pharaoh and all his household are afflicted with plagues;[23] and when the cause of their suffering is revealed, the monarch—with what may be regarded as justifiable consternation—asks what possible explanation Abram might have for his deception. No words are recorded in the patriarch's defense, however; and he and his household are expelled under guard (12:17–20).

Some time later, YHWH addresses the patriarch in a vision: "Fear not, Abram," the Lord says. "I am a shield to you; your reward shall be very great" (15:1). Abram's frankly human response expresses his doubt and resignation. "O Lord GOD, what can You give me," he asks, "seeing that I shall die childless" (15:2). YHWH answers, however, by taking Abram outside and promising that his offspring will be as numerous as the stars of the heavens (15:5). God has pledged that Abram's heir will be "none but your very own issue" (15:4; see also 13:14–18). But will Sarai bear that child, or will some other, fertile woman share with Abram in God's promise?

Sarai and Hagar

The story of Hagar, Sarai's Egyptian handmaiden, begins in Genesis 16 and resumes in Genesis 21:9–20. These are tragic traditions, to be sure; and they have created untoward problems for interpreters, ancient and modern. At present, we shall touch upon them only briefly, because Hagar's story deserves close scrutiny within a chapter that bears her own name. In the next chapter, we shall explore the tragedy of Sarai's dealings with Hagar, but we shall also ask what responsibility, if any, Abram must bear for Hagar's suffering. Why do most commentators exonerate him, yet indict Sarai?

Genesis 16 begins with two statements of fact: Sarai is barren, and she has an Egyptian maidservant named Hagar. She therefore resolves to give Hagar to Abram in order that she may claim as her own the children born of their union. Such a solution may strike us as unsavory, but it was not an innovation on Sarai's part. On the contrary, it conformed to ancient Near Eastern familial law.

The strategy works; Hagar conceives. When her attitude toward her mistress changes, however, Sarai receives Abram's permission to reassert her control over Hagar. Sarai becomes abusive, and the Egyptian woman flees from her mistress, setting out through the desert for Egypt, her home. But her escape is checked by a messenger of YHWH, who orders her back to her mistress with the promise that her offspring, too, will be innumerable. Hagar returns and bears a son whom Abram names Ishmael. Abram is eighty-six years old when the baby is born.

Laughing at God's Promise of a Son

Thirteen years later, YHWH appears to Abram once more, repeating the covenant promises, changing his name from Abram to Abraham,[24] and instituting male circumcision as the sign of their covenant bond. Next, God speaks of Sarai:

> [15]As for your wife Sarai, you shall not call her Sarai, but her name shall be Sarah.[25] [16]I will bless her; indeed, I will give you a son by her. I will bless her so that she shall give rise to nations; rulers of peoples shall issue from her (Gen. 17:15–16).

Abram's response to this announcement is, at best, unceremonious: He falls on his face and laughs, thinking, "Can a child be born to a man a hundred years old, or can Sarah bear a child at ninety?" (17:17). Abraham laughs at the promise of a child? Many readers are astonished to discover such a thing. They know only of Sarah's famous laugh in the following chapter. Yet here, in the presence of the Lord, Abraham laughs first. To be sure, chapter 17 is the product of the priestly writers and so, in its canonical form at least, postdates the earlier material found in Genesis 18.[26] Nonetheless, in its canonical form, laughing Abraham precedes laughing Sarah, so one can at least wonder why the latter story is so famous, the former so often overlooked.[27]

Sarah's next and best known appearance is described in Genesis 18. When the episode begins, Abraham is sitting at the entrance of the tent; Sarah is inside. The biblical narrator informs us that it is a hot time of the day, but he does not indicate how many days have passed since the events of chapter 17 occurred. The rabbis filled in this gap, however, explaining that it was the third day since Abraham's circumcision. The patriarch was, understandably, in great pain, so God drilled a hole into hell in order that its heat might reach the earth and discourage wayfarers from disturbing him. God apparently did not think that a divine visit would be an inconvenience, however, for the Lord said to the angels, "Go to, let us pay a visit to the sick."[28]

Suddenly, Abraham sees three men standing near him. Immediately he runs to greet them, bowing to the ground and urging them to accept his hospitality.[29] His words convey a sense of urgency and excitement: "My lords, if it please you, do not go on past your servant. Let a little water be brought; bathe your feet and recline under the tree. And let me fetch a morsel of bread that you may refresh yourselves; then go on—seeing that you have come your servant's way" (18:3b–5a).

"Do as you have said," his visitors reply (18:5b), and Abraham springs into action. Darting into the tent, he orders Sarah, "Quick, three *seahs* of choice flour! Knead and make cakes!" Next, he personally selects a choice calf and gives it to a servant-boy to prepare.[30] Finally, he takes

curds and milk and the prepared calf and sets them before his guests, waiting on them as they eat beneath the
tree. "Where is your wife Sarah?" they ask (18:9); when
Abraham replies that she is in the tent, one of his guests
makes a startling announcement: "I will return to you
next year, and your wife Sarah shall have a son!" (18:10)[31]

Now, the narrator informs us that Sarah has overheard
the visitor's declaration, for she is listening at the entrance to the tent. He also pauses to let us know that
Abraham and Sarah are old, and she no longer has
monthly periods (18:11).[32] Sarah laughs to herself at the
thought of a pregnancy: "Now that I am withered, am I
to have enjoyment—with my husband so old?" (18:12).
Her laughter does not go unnoticed:

> [13]Then the Lord said to Abraham, "Why did Sarah
> laugh, saying, 'Shall I in truth bear a child, old as I
> am?' [14]Is anything too wondrous for the Lord?[33] I will
> return to you at the time next year, and Sarah shall
> have a son." [15]Sarah lied, saying, "I did not laugh," for
> she was frightened. But He replied, "You did laugh"
> (Gen. 18:13–15).

This text has afforded some commentators an opportunity to criticize Sarah. Von Rad, for example, speaks of
Sarah's "unbelieving and perhaps somewhat evil
laugh."[34] Certainly, Sarah's incredulity earned her a censure from their guest, although it was, ostensibly, no
more noxious than Abraham's own response to the divine
promise in Genesis 17.

Who are these three visitors? Their identity is difficult
to determine, because the text is somewhat confusing on
this point. The chapter begins with the phrase, "*The Lord*
appeared to him [Abraham] by the terebinths of
Mamre." But Abraham's reaction is to the sudden appearance of *three men*. In the following exchanges, these
three guests either speak together (18:5, 9), or one of the
three speaks, but they are not identified (18:10). In verse

13, however, the text clearly states that "*the LORD* said to Abraham." How can we understand this inconsistency? Early Christians found in our text a reference to the Holy Trinity, and von Rad may be influenced by this view when he suggests that YHWH in fact appears in the person of all three guests. He must admit, however, that such a notion is "so strange and singular in the Old Testament that it must belong to the peculiarity of this tradition and this tradition only.[35] More helpful is his recognition that behind our text lies a type of story, common in the ancient world, in which deities visit human beings on earth. The biblical narrator has adopted such a story and altered it (18:1, 13) to make it palatable to his Israelite audience, but he has not eliminated the tensions that are thereby created.

Rabbinical Reflections on Genesis 18:1–15

Like modern critics, the rabbis noticed that the Lord's appearance to Abraham at Mamre and the arrival of the three men were not easily understood as the same event. They resolved this difficulty, however, by interpreting them as sequential visitations. First God, accompanied by a host of angels, appeared to Abraham. The patriarch naturally attempted to stand up as a sign of respect, but the Lord dissuaded him on account of his painful condition. When Abraham saw the three men, he did not realize that they were angels—Michael, Gabriel, and Raphael. He nevertheless excused himself from God's presence because, the rabbis taught, "he considered the duty of hospitality more important than the duty of receiving the Shekinah."[36]

They further noted that Abraham—one of those truly pious individuals "who promise little, but perform much"—offered his guests only a morsel of bread (v. 5), but prepared a banquet fit for King Solomon himself.

Contrary to the biblical text, Abraham slaughtered three calves, not just one. He could, therefore, serve a "tongue with mustard" to each of his guests. His explicit instructions to Sarah that she use three *seahs* of choice flour was necessary, the rabbis said, because Abraham knew that women tend to be stingy with guests.[37] Although Sarah prepared the bread as instructed, the text does not say that Abraham actually gave it to his guests along with the curds, milk, and meat. Some rabbis insisted that the bread was served nonetheless, for "if he brought them what he had not offered, [curds and milk] how much more what he had offered!" A dissenting opinion held, however, that Sarah became menstruous while she was baking, so the dough was rendered unclean.[38] Although we read in the Bible that "[Abraham] waited on them under the tree *as they ate*" (18:8), the rabbis insisted that they did not actually consume any food. Instead, "the portions set before the angels were devoured by a heavenly fire."[39]

Lest anyone conclude that the question "Where is your wife Sarah?" was uttered out of ignorance, the rabbis explained that these angels knew perfectly well where Sarah was. They inquired after her out of respect, intending to send her a cup of wine over which a blessing had been recited. It was Michael, the most eminent of the angels, who revealed to Sarah that she would bear a son. Yes, the revelation was actually intended for *her* ears, since Abraham already had received the good news (17:19). Yet because it would not have been seemly for him to have a private communication with a man's wife, Michael stood at the entrance to the tent, and Ishmael stationed himself between the angel and Sarah.[40]

Since the rabbis believed that both God and the three angels were present with Abraham, they simply understood the question, "Why did Sarah laugh?" to be the Lord's first contribution to the conversation. In their view, the reproach inherent in the query was intended for Abraham as well, since he also laughed when Isaac's birth was foretold to him (17:17). But while God reproached Sarah explicitly, Abraham was left to "become conscious of his defect himself."[41]

Finally, the rabbis discerned in God's remarks a slight distortion. After all, Sarah had said, "Now that I am withered, am I to have enjoyment—*with my husband so old?* (18:12, emphasis added). When the Lord repeated Sarah's words, however ("Why did Sarah laugh, saying, 'Shall I in truth bear a child, *old as I am?*' " emphasis added), the reference to age was transferred to her. Why did the Lord misrepresent Sarah's speech? Because, the rabbis explained, "Abraham might have taken amiss what his wife had said about his advanced years, and so precious is the peace between husband and wife that even the Holy One, blessed be He, preserved it at the expense of truth."[42]

Sarah in the Harem of Abimelech

Sarah does not appear in the scenes immediately following the announcement that she will bear a child. She is not witness to Abraham's intercession with God on behalf of Sodom (Gen. 18:22–33). On the following morning, Sarah is not depicted as rushing with Abraham to the elevated place where the cities of Sodom and Gomorrah, now reduced to smoldering ruins, can be seen. Only when Abraham travels to the southwest, sojourning in Gerar, does she reappear in a scene not unlike one we have witnessed before; again, Abraham claims that Sarah is his sister, and the ruler of the region, Abimelech, orders that she be brought into his harem (20:1–3).[43]

Unlike the story of Sarah and Pharaoh (part of the Yahwistic source), the account of Sarah and King Abimelech of Gerar is widely regarded as the product of the Elohist. As noted above, many biblical scholars believe that these two stories are actually different renditions of a single tradition.[44] When a later redactor included the Elohist's version as a second, separate episode, however, its insertion at this much later point in the cycle created a difficulty: Since no reason is given for Abimelech's desire to possess Sarah, we will likely assume that her beauty motivated him, as it had Pharaoh (12:11–15). Yet by this point in the narrative, Sarah is at least ninety years old!

Although the plot line of the two episodes in which Sarah is imperiled is essentially the same—the matriarch, who has been identified as Abraham's sister, is taken into a foreign ruler's harem, the deception is discovered, and Abraham and Sarah depart, all the richer for the experience—a careful reader will discover many differences between them as well.[45] Unlike the Yahwist, for example, the Elohist is unwilling to leave open the question of whether her abductor had sexual intercourse with Sarah. Rather, he states explicitly that "Abimelech had not approached her" (20:4; see also v. 6). He likewise specifies that the King of Gerar learned Sarah's true identity from the Lord, who spoke to him in a dream.[46] Abimelech's life can be saved, God informs him, if he restores Sarah to her husband, because Abraham is a prophet and, as such, can successfully intercede on the King's behalf.[47] Like Pharaoh, Abimelech is aghast at Abraham's deception and demands to know the reason for his behavior. Yet here, too, the Elohist differs from the Yahwist in that he is careful to explain and justify the patriarch's conduct. A surprising element in Abraham's defense is his insistence that Sarah is, in fact, his half-sister: " 'I thought,' said Abraham, 'surely there is no fear of God in this place, and they will kill me because of my wife. And besides, she is in truth my sister, my father's daughter though not my mother's; and she became my wife' " (20:11–12).

Here is quite an unexpected revelation. When their names first appeared in the genealogy of Genesis 11, there was no hint that Abram and Sarai were siblings.[48] Moreover, such a union would be a violation of later Israelite law, which explicitly forbade sexual relationships between siblings, including half-siblings (Lev. 18:9, 20:17; Deut. 27:22). Did Abraham simply offer Abimelech an explanation that he could accept, because it conformed to the social practices of that region? Such is the view preserved in *Midrash Rabbah*: "He answered them in accordance with their own views, for they permit [marriage with] the daughter of one's father, but interdict the daughter of one's mother."[49] In the Talmud we read yet another explanation: Sarah was actually the daughter of Abraham's brother—more specifically, a brother with whom Abraham shared the same father, but not the same mother.[50] Clearly, the rabbis struggled to explain how Abraham's apparent breach of Torah was, in fact, no violation at all. A few contemporary scholars have wondered, however, whether 20:11–12 actually reflects an ancient practice of tracing blood lines matrilineally (through the mother), rather than patrilineally, so that persons sharing only the same father were not regarded as blood relatives.[51]

According to the rabbis, Abraham's petition on behalf of Abimelech's household was the first successful intercessory prayer in the history of the world. So efficacious were Abraham's words that Abimelech's wife, who was unable to have children even before Abraham and Sarah entered Gerar, conceived and gave birth to a child. This miracle elicted from the angels a mighty protest, for they said, "O Lord of the world! All these years hath Sarah been barren, as the wife of Abimelech was. Now Abraham prayed to Thee, and the wife of Abimelech hath been granted a child. It is just and fair that Sarah should be remembered and granted a child."[52]

Sarah Has a Son

In Genesis 21, we read at last of the long-awaited birth of Sarah's son. The babe is born at the exact time fore-

told by God,[53] and Abraham names him Isaac. When the
infant is eight days old, he is circumcised by his father.
"God has brought me laughter," Sarah says. "Everyone
who hears will laugh with me." Then she adds, "Who
would have said to Abraham that Sarah would suckle children![54] Yet I have borne a son in his old age" (21:6–7).[55]
According to Jewish legend, Isaac's birth initiated a period of universal elation:

> The whole world rejoiced, for God remembered all
> barren women at the same time with Sarah. They all
> bore children. And all the blind were made to see, all
> the lame were made whole, the dumb were made to
> speak, and the mad were restored to reason.[56]

But why was the world forced to wait so long for this
wonderful, healing nativity? Because, the rabbis explained, it was necessary that Abraham be circumcised
before Isaac, the father of Israel, could be conceived. In
order to preclude any doubt that Abraham had sired this
child, they added, the Lord commanded the angel in
charge of human embryos to form the baby in the very
image of his father.[57]

The Expulsion of Hagar and Ishmael

Isaac's weaning is an occasion for celebration indeed,
since many an infant of the ancient world did not survive
to reach that milestone. Abraham therefore hosts a lavish
party. In the midst of the festivities, however, Sarah per-
ceives that Ishmael poses a threat to Isaac's inheritance.
She therefore orders Abraham to cast out both Hagar
and his firstborn son. According to the biblical text,
Sarah's demand troubled her husband, "for it concerned
a son of his" (Gen. 21:11). But God sides with Sarah in
the dispute, insisting that Isaac is the son who will con-

tinue his line. "As for the son of the slave-woman," God adds, "I will make a nation of him, too, for he is your seed" (21:13).

Early next morning Abraham gives Hagar bread and water and sends mother and son away. They wander in the wilderness of Beer-sheba until their water is gone, and Ishmael begins to suffer from thirst. At length, Hagar places him under a bush and sits some distance away, thinking "Let me not look on as the child dies" (21:16). YHWH is aware of their distress, however; and a divine messenger calls to Hagar, instructing her to "lift up the boy and hold him by the hand, for I will make a great nation of him." Suddenly, Hagar spies a well. She draws water for her son, who drinks it and is revived. Ishmael grows up to become a bowman, living in the desert of Paran. And as her last recorded act, Hagar secures for her son an Egyptian wife.

Authorized by God though it be, Sarah's role in the expulsion of Hagar and Ishmael has earned her a solid rebuke from many commentators. Indeed, the story is told in a way that elicits sympathy for Hagar and Ishmael, and even for Abraham, at Sarah's expense.[58] As we shall see in the next chapter, the rabbis sought to defend her behavior to some degree. Yet even they felt forced, at points, to concede Sarah's guilt in the matter of Hagar and Ishmael.

The Binding of Isaac

Sarah's name does not appear in Genesis 22, the story of Abraham's faithful and terrifying obedience to God's command that he sacrifice Isaac atop Mount Moriah.[59] The rabbis did not fail to link her to her son's near demise, however, in at least two ways. On the one hand, some commentators regarded the binding of Isaac as Abraham and Sarah's punishment for the sufferings of

Hagar and Ishmael. On the other hand, they claimed that Sarah's own passing was linked directly to her son's brush with death.

In Genesis 22:1, the biblical narrator tells his readers something that Abraham does not yet know. "Some time afterward," he says, "God *put* Abraham *to the test*" (emphasis added). This test, for which no motive is immediately given, consists of a horrific command: "Take your son, your only son Isaac, whom you love, and go to the land of Moriah, and offer him there as a burnt offering upon one of the mountains of which I shall tell you" (22:2, RSV). Early the next morning, Abraham, Isaac, and two young servants set off on the three-day journey. When Moriah is in sight, Abraham orders the attendants to remain where they are while he and Isaac continue on together. Arriving at their destination, Abraham builds an altar, arranges the wood, binds his son, and places him upon the altar. Knife in hand, he is about to slay Isaac when a messenger of YHWH stops him, explaining that his willingness to make this sacrifice proves that he fears God (22:12) and is obedient to God's commands (22:18).

Genesis 22 is a powerful, moving, and suspenseful story. A literary masterpiece, its rhetorical power is due, in part, to its laconic narrative style. For example, what follows is the only recorded conversation between father and son during their entire journey:

ISAAC: "Father!"
ABRAHAM: "Yes, my son."
ISAAC: "Here are the firestone and the wood, but where is the sheep for the burnt offering?"
ABRAHAM: "God will see to the sheep for His burnt offering, my son."

(after Gen. 22:7–8a)

In their commentaries, however, the rabbis elaborated upon the story. They believed, for example, that Abraham told Isaac what the Lord was requiring of him. Isaac consented to the sacrifice, but he urged his father to tie him tightly lest he, out of weakness and love of life, resist at the last moment. Faced with death, Isaac's thoughts turned to his mother. He therefore said to Abraham:

Turn up thy garment, gird thy loins, and after that thou hast slaughtered me, burn me into fine ashes. Then gather the ashes, and bring them to Sarah, my mother, and place them in a casket in her chamber. At all hours, whenever she enters her chamber, she will remember her son Isaac and weep for him.[60]

Although the biblical text specifically claims that Isaac was not sacrificed, there is no mention of his returning with his father to the spot where the two servants were left behind. Verse 19 states only that "Abraham returned to his young men, and they arose and went together to Beer-sheba; and Abraham dwelt at Beer-sheba." Where was Isaac? In paradise, the rabbis replied. True, Abraham did not kill him. But angels transported Isaac there all the same, and he remained in paradise for three years before returning to earth.[61]

Sarah's Death

The death of Sarah at one hundred and twenty-seven years is recorded in Genesis 23, the chapter following the account of Isaac's near-fatal experience at Moriah.[62] For the rabbis, the juxtaposition of these two events was not coincidental. When Abraham received God's command to sacrifice his son, they explained, he lied to Sarah, telling her that they were only traveling to a place where Isaac could study Torah. Sarah's heart was broken at the thought of a separation from her child. She spent the entire evening embracing him and offering advice. The next morning, Sarah dressed Isaac in one of the beautiful garments that King Abimelech had given her. She accompanied her husband and son on the road, but eventually Abraham told her to return to the tent. Sarah burst into tears; and soon everyone, including the two servants, was weeping. At length, Sarah embraced Isaac, saying "Who knoweth if I shall ever see thee again after this day?"[63]

According to one Jewish legend, Satan disguised himself as an old man and visited Sarah shortly after Abraham and Isaac's departure.[64] He told her Abraham's true reason for taking Isaac, and Sarah wept bitterly, utterly a lament-*cum*-prayer:

"O my son, Isaac, my son, O that I had this day died instead of thee! It grieves me for thee! After that I have reared thee and have brought thee up, my joy is turned into mourning over thee. In my longing for a child, I cried and prayed, till I bore thee at ninety. Now hast thou served this day for the knife and the fire. But I console myself, it being the word of God, and thou didst perform the command of thy God, for who can transgress the word of our God, in whose hands is the soul of every living creature? Thou art just, O Lord our God, for all Thy works are good and righteous, for I also rejoice with the word which Thou didst command, and while mine eye weepeth bitterly, my heart rejoiceth."[65]

Setting out, Sarah asked everyone she met for some news about her son, but no one could tell her anything. Finally, when Sarah had traveled as far as Hebron, Satan again appeared to her as an old man and said, "I spoke falsely unto thee, for Abraham did not kill his son, and he is not dead." When Sarah heard this news, she was so filled with joy that "her soul went out" and she perished.[66]

When Sarah died, the Bible says, "Abraham proceeded to mourn for Sarah and to bewail her." Modern commentators are quick to point out that this verse tells us

little about Abraham's actual emotional response to
Sarah's passing, since mourning and bewailing were "for-
mal rites, which [had] no bearing, one way or another, on
the survivor's personal feelings."[67] The rabbis expounded
upon the grief occasioned by Sarah's death, however,
noting that Abraham was so overwhelmed with sorrow
that, for once, he could not pray. The loss of Sarah sad-
dened not only his household, but also the whole
country:

> So long as she was alive, all went well in the land. After
> her death confusion ensued. The weeping, lamenting,
> and wailing over her going hence was universal, and
> Abraham, instead of receiving consolation, had to of-
> fer consolation to others.[68]

Sarah's Burial at Machpelah

Sarah is the first of Abraham's family to die in the land
of Canaan, and the patriarch needs a place to bury her.
The purchase of Machpelah, a field near Mamre that included a cave, is detailed in Genesis 23:3–20; and despite
the solemnity of the occasion, the transaction is not without its humorous notes. Because he is a resident alien in
the land, Abraham must first appeal to the Hittites (literally, the "children of Heth") for a burial site. Their leaders respond graciously: "Hear us, my lord: you are the
elect of God among us. Bury your dead in the choicest of
our burial places; none of us will withhold his burial place
from you for burying your dead" (23:6). Abraham wishes
clear title to the property, however; and so he asks the
council to intercede on his behalf with Ephron, son of
Zohar and owner of Machpelah. Ephron, too, is extremely gracious—so much so that we begin to suspect
that his words are the requisite, effusive rhetoric that precedes the real business at hand:

[10]Ephron was present among the Hittites; so Ephron the Hittite answered Abraham in the hearing of the Hittites, all who entered the gate of his town, saying [11]"No, my lord, hear me: I give you the field and I give you the cave that is in it; I give it to you in the presence of my people. Bury your dead." [12]Then Abraham bowed low before the people of the land, [13]and spoke to Ephron in the hearing of the people of the land, saying, "If only you would hear me out! Let me pay the price of the land; accept it from me, that I may bury my dead there." [14]Ephron replied to Abraham, saying to him, [15]"My lord, do hear me! A piece of land worth four hundred shekels of silver—what is that between you and me? Go and bury your dead" (Gen. 23:10–15).

Ah, ha! At last Ephron has played his hand. The price of the field will be four hundred pieces of silver, probably an exorbitant amount. Abraham accepts the offer, however; and Sarah is laid to rest.

In the Bible, the cave at Machpelah was the final resting place not only of Sarah, but also of Abraham, Isaac and Rebekah, and Jacob and Leah. According to Jewish tradition, however, Adam and Eve also were buried there. Abraham had discovered them, reclining upon couches beside an eternal flame, when he entered the cave to catch a stray ox. It was for that reason, the rabbis said, that he wanted to purchase that particular property. When he placed Sarah inside the cave, Adam and Eve tried to leave because, they said, "as it is, we are ashamed in the presence of God on account of the sin we committed, and now we shall be even more ashamed on account of your good deeds." Abraham comforted Adam, however, by promising to pray on his behalf.[69]

Abraham lived approximately forty-eight years beyond the death of Sarah. He married again and, with Keturah, his wife, had six more children. Death came at the age of one hundred and seventy-five. According to the rabbis,

Sarah also should have lived that long, but her life was cut short as punishment for an unbridled utterance:

> R. Tanchuma said in the name of R. Hiyya the elder, and R. Berekiah said in R. Eleazar's name: Whoever plunges eagerly into litigation does not escape from it unscathed. Sarah should have reached Abraham's years, but because she said, THE LORD JUDGE BE-TWEEN ME AND THEE,[70] her life was reduced by forty-eight years.[71]

Sarah as a Symbol of Hope

At the beginning of this chapter, we noted that the biblical Abraham and Sarah traditions were composed and combined at different periods of Israel's history. It is clear that the people involved in the creation and transmission of the pentateuchal traditions cared that Sarah's story, and other stories of Israel's earliest ancestors, be preserved and cherished by their descendants.

When we look beyond the Pentateuch, however, we find only one other explicit reference to Sarah, the wife of Abraham, in the entire Hebrew Bible. Her memory is not recalled by the psalmists, and no prophet refers to her until we come to the Second Isaiah collection (Isaiah 40–55). Only then, when her descendants again find themselves in the most barren and hopeless of circumstances, is Sarah's story lifted up by a prophet who perceived in "the creation of Israel out of Sarah's barren womb" a paradigm for "the new creation of Israel out of the desolate Jerusalem."[72] If God could bring new life out of barren Sarah, was anything too wondrous for the Lord? "Look back to Abraham your father and to Sarah

who brought you forth" (Isa. 51:2a), Second Isaiah said,
for he (or she) understood well the power of remembering where you came from. Some fellow exiles had forgotten their old traditions, their ancient inheritance. And so,
of course, they had forgotten what those traditions could
teach them about themselves and, most of all, about their
God. Had they remembered their stories, those exiles
would have realized that theirs was not the first generation of Israelites to find itself in what looked like a hopeless situation. On the contrary, they had been birthed in
impossibility and sustained against all odds. Certainly, a
people who claimed as their ancestor a baby born to a
ninety-year-old post-menopausal woman should have expected to stretch the odds a bit, should they not?

To the exiles who had forgotten these things, Second
Isaiah told stories, including the story of Sarah and Abraham. He reminded them of their beginnings—not so
they could console themselves by retreating from reality,
but rather to convince them that just as YHWH had given
a son to this barren woman of old, so God's presence was
given to them now. What God did for Sarah was evidence
of what God was doing, and would continue to do, for
the exiles.

And so, deep in the heart of Babylon, deep in the midst
of exile, an anonymous prophet evoked memory of a very
old tradition in order to describe the future of God's
people:

> ¹Shout, O barren one,
> You who bore no child!
> Shout aloud for joy,
> You who did not travail!
> For the children of the wife forlorn
> Shall outnumber those of the espoused
>
> —said the LORD.
>
> ²Enlarge the site of your tent,
> Extend the size of your dwelling,

Do not stint!
Lengthen the ropes, and drive the pegs firm.

³For you shall spread out to the right and the left;
Your offspring shall dispossess nations
And shall people the desolate towns (Isa. 54:1–3).[73]

He proclaimed that,

²⁰The children you thought you had lost
Shall yet say in your hearing,
"The place is too crowded for me;
Make room for me to settle."

²¹And you will say to yourself,
"Who bore these for me
When I was bereaved and barren,
Exiled and disdained—
By whom, then, were these reared?
I was left all alone—
And where have these been?" (Isa. 49:20–21).

You see, Second Isaiah says, the God of Abraham and
Sarah is also the God who is with us, here in Babylonian
exile. In this time of despair and hopelessness, God is
present with us. Do not fear, he seems to say, for soon,
our barrenness shall be so transformed that Jerusalem
will become an ancient version of the old woman who
lived in a shoe and had so many children, she didn't know
what to do!

Sarah and the Rabbis

For the rabbis, too, Sarah was a symbol of hope.
Like Second Isaiah and his successors, the authors of

Isaiah 56–66, the rabbis linked Zion's future with Sarah, affirming that just as God had given a son to her (and to the other barren matriarchs of the Bible), so also would Jerusalem's barrenness be relieved by the birth of children.[74] Moreover, certain of their elaborations upon the Sarah stories indicate that they perceived in Sarah a presage of the world to come. Remember, for example, their affirmation that, when Isaac was born, blind eyes were opened, the lame were healed, mutes were able to speak, and reason returned to the insane? For the rabbis, such healings prefigured that day when the present age would come to an end and a glorious new age would begin.[75]

They did not intend, however, that Sarah's story be limited to expressions of hope for the future alone. Rather, the rabbis were concerned to show that scripture, including the barren matriarch traditions, had immediate relevance for people struggling to live faithfully in the here and now.[76] More than a Bronze Age relic or a portent of the future, Sarah was a model for faithful Jewish living. When Abram and Sarai were in Haran, for example, and Abraham busied himself converting the heathen to Judaism, Sarai was right beside him, converting the women.[77] Despite her great beauty, she remained modest and loyal to her husband. Moreover, in times of trouble she, like the other biblical matriarchs, prayed to God, and the Lord took pleasure in her prayers.[78] It was on account of her good deeds, therefore, that Sarah was relieved of the onus of barrenness and granted a child. In *Midrash Rabbah* we read:

> R. Adda said: "The Holy One, blessed be He, is a trustee: Amalek deposited with Him bundles of thorns [wrongdoings]; therefore He returned to him bundles of thorns [punishment], as it says, *I remember that which Amalek did to Israel* (1 Sam. xv, 2). Sarah laid up with Him a store of pious acts and good deeds; therefore the Lord returned her [the reward for] these, as it says, AND THE LORD REMEMBERED SARAH.[79]

To be sure, rabbinical commentators could, on occasion, be critical of Sarah. They claimed, for example, that she shared the natural propensity of women to be selfish with guests, to eavesdrop, and to be slothful.[80] Neither was she blameless in her treatment of Hagar and Ishmael. Nevertheless, they esteemed her highly. In the Talmud, Sarah is first among the seven biblical prophetesses.[81] Indeed, her prophetic powers were said to have exceeded those of her husband, for she was able to discern God's will in expelling Hagar and Ishmael, while Abraham resisted until the Lord ordered, "whatever Sarah tells you, do as she says."[82]

Feminist Perspectives on Sarah

Contemporary women do not speak with a single voice about Sarah. This is scarcely surprising, for women, like men, bring their own presuppositions, experiences, and perspectives to these traditions; and what they bring inevitably influences to some degree what they take away from the text. This does not mean, of course, that the text does not constrain certain interpretations. It would, for example, be difficult to claim that Sarah was so much the victim of her patriarchal culture that she was powerless to speak her mind regardless of the circumstances, for such a view flies in the face of texts like Genesis 16:5 and 21:10. Nevertheless, within the boundaries of responsible reading, one finds a great number of perspectives from women who have looked back to Sarah. In this section, we shall deal briefly with three different interpretations. However, our reflections must remain preliminary at this point, for contemporary feminist and womanist perspectives on Sarah have been greatly affected by her interactions with Hagar and Ishmael, and we shall not deal fully with those traditions until chapter four.

Janice Nunnally-Cox is among recent interpreters who are impressed by the power that Sarah wields in some of the biblical stories.[83] She notes that, as Sarai and Abram are approaching Egypt, he does not order her to comply with his planned deception. Rather, Abraham must ask her to say that she is his sister. He cohabits with Hagar because Sarah wants him to; and when she decides that Ishmael is a threat to her own son's inheritance, Sarah succeeds in expelling both mother and child. Indeed, God defends her demand; and this is not the only time that the Lord acts on Sarah's behalf. In Pharaoh's court, and within the household of Abimelech, God is concerned that Sarah be protected and returned to her husband. "It is to the writer's credit," Nunnally-Cox writes, "that he would interpret the happenings to a woman's influence."[84] True, Sarah is severely criticized by God for laughing at the announcement of her future pregnancy. Nevertheless, Nunnally-Cox believes that, given their social context, Sarah and Abraham are amazingly equal:

> She appears to say what she wants, when she wants, and Abraham at times responds in almost meek obedience. He does not command her; she commands him, yet there seems to be an affectionate bond between them. Abraham does not abandon Sarah during her barrenness, nor does he gain other wives while she lives, as far as we know. The two have grown up together and grown old together, and when Sarah dies, Abraham can do nothing but weep. Sarah is a matriarch of the first order: respected by rulers and husbands alike, a spirited woman and bold companion.[85]

Against such a reading, Esther Fuchs argues that biblical mothers, Sarah among them, are depicted in ways that advance the patriarchal concerns of the narrators.[86] Central among those concerns, Fuchs says, is man's control

of female sexuality and reproductive capacity. The institution of motherhood is a "powerful patriarchal mecha-
nism" for retaining that control:[87]

> Male control of female reproductive powers in con-
> junction with patrilocal and monogamous marriage
> (for the wife), secures the wife as her husband's exclu-
> sive property and ensures the continuity of his name
> and family possessions through patrinomial customs
> and patrilineal inheritance patterns. The institution of
> motherhood as defined by the patriarchal system guar-
> antees that both the wife and her children will increase
> his property during his lifetime and perpetuate his
> achievements and memory after his death.[88]

Fuchs identifies rhetorical strategies employed in the
narratives to drive home these values and concerns. She
also notes ways by which the narrator narrows the range
of Sarah's experiences. Although Abraham appears in a
variety of scenes and situations, Sarah is present mainly
in episodes related to her sexual and reproductive capabilities. Even when she does appear, however, the narrative may have little interest in her. The real foci of the
two "endangered matriarch" stories, for example, are the
threat that Abraham's reproductive "vessel" will pass out
of his control and cease to increase his material wealth.
Sarah's response to these situations is nowhere recorded.

This marginalization of the matriarch is particularly apparent in the annunciation scene in Genesis 18. According to verse 1, YHWH appears to Abraham, not to Sarah.[89]
When three guests visit, Abraham is the active agent;
Sarah remains sequestered in the tent and obeys his orders. Concealed behind the tent entrance, Sarah must
listen while these "men" discuss her reproductive future.
For Fuchs, her twice-mentioned absence (18:6, 9) is not
without significance: "The literary constellation of male
characters surrounding and determining the fate of the
potential mother dramatizes the idea that woman's repro-

ductive potential should be and can be controlled only by
men.''[90] Indeed, Sarah's only contribution to the scene is
a disruption, and when she laughs, she earns her only
direct communication with the visitor—a rebuke. In
short, Fuchs concludes, "Sarah emerges from the scene
as confined, passive, cowardly, deceptive, and above all
untrusting of YHWH's omnipotence. Sarah's participation
in the annunciation type-scene amounts to a troublesome
interference. She is not only inferior to Abraham in the
literary sense, as a secondary character, but in a moral
and spiritual sense, as well."[91]

When Isaac is born, it is Abraham who names and cir-
cumcises him; and he hosts the feast that celebrates his
weaning. Sarah, for her part, behaves in ways consistent
with other biblical mothers. First and foremost, she is
concerned for her son's well-being,[92] and that central
preoccupation places her in an antagonistic relationship
with another female, Hagar, resulting in the expulsion of
them both:

> The motif of motherhood in the biblical narrative
> seems to be closely associated with the motif of female
> rivalry. The mother-harlot who steals her roommate's
> son away and encourages the king to kill him acts on
> the same motivation that drove Sarah to drive out Ha-
> gar and her son Ishmael (Gen. 21:9–10). . . . By per-
> petuating the theme of woman's mutual rivalry,
> especially in a reproductive context, the narrative im-
> plies that sisterhood is a precarious alternative to the
> patriarchal system.[93]

Through various rhetorical strategies, then, the biblical
narrative seeks to inculcate patriarchal values and to per-
petuate male control over females. That it succeeds in
doing so while creating the illusion that it is simply a
neutral description of reality is, as Fuchs observes, a testi-
mony to the narrator's literary skill.[94]

Savina Teubal, author of *Sarah the Priestess,* also recognizes the patriarchal cast of the biblical traditions about Israel's early ancestors. She believes, however, that in their original forms, these stories reflected a matriarchal culture struggling to survive its encounter with patriarchy and Yahwism.

Teubal's interest is piqued by some unusual features of the biblical ancestral traditions: Why was not Sarai's marriage to Abram regarded as incestuous? Why does her burial at Mamre receive so much attention? Why did Isaac consummate his marriage to Rebekah in his mother's tent? Why, in the stories of Israel's patriarchs and matriarchs, does the youngest son so often become the heir? These and other questions kick off a fascinating, highly imaginative reconstruction of the life of Sarah and her successors, Rebekah, Leah, and Rachel. Drawing upon a diverse collection of extra-biblical witnesses, as well as her ability to "read between the lines" of the biblical traditions, Teubal argues that the Mesopotamian wives of the patriarchs brought with them to Canaan their matriarchal culture and religion. Although Abraham and his male descendants quickly succumbed to the patriarchal ways of Canaanite society, Sarah and her successors resisted the loss of their social and religious authority. That their power was not easily supplanted is suggested by vestiges of matriarchy that have survived within the biblical traditions: the acceptance of marriage between nonuterine siblings (like Abram and Sarah, Gen. 20:12); ultimogeniture, according to which the youngest child, and not the oldest, inherits (e.g., Jacob); and matrilocal marriage (i.e., the husband resides with his wife's family).[95]

It was because of Sarah, Teubal argues, that Abraham chose to settle at the sacred terebinths of Mamre. There, his wife functioned as a priestess who, like the Babylonian *en* and *naditu,* was not permitted to have children.[96] Although her marriage to Abraham was a celibate union, Teubal conjectures that Sarah had intercourse with other men on two (12:10–20; 20:1–18) and perhaps three

(18:1–15) occasions. These copulations were not the illicit acts of an adulterous wife; rather, they were ritual performances of the *hieros gamos,* a sacred marriage rite performed by a priestess (the incarnation of the goddess) and kings as "the test and confirmation of a ruler's virility, which would ensure abundance to the land and the people."[97] It was during the ritual with Abimelech, Teubal believes, that Isaac was conceived—to Sarah's utter astonishment, since she believed Abimelech to be sterile (20:17).

Careful readers will undoubtedly note that Teubal's argument, particularly as it pertains to Sarah's priestly functions and their outcome, relies very heavily upon "possible" scenarios, arguments from silence, and sheer speculation. She treats the Sarah traditions sometimes as myths, sometimes as accurate descriptions of actual historical accounts. Moreover, her use of geographically and chronologically diverse ancient Near Eastern texts is haphazard and methodologically problematic. Nevertheless, Teubal's study of the ancestral traditions in light of matriarchal social practices is suggestive at points, for there are elements of these stories that are better understood in light of at least parts of her reconstruction. In any event, Teubal's book helps us read Israel's ancestral traditions with a new appreciation for the importance of Sarah and her successors:

> The narratives of the Sarah tradition represent a non-patriarchal system struggling for survival in isolation in a foreign land. Nevertheless, women of strength emerge from the pages of Genesis, women who are respected by men. Their function in life, though different from that of men, is regarded as equally important to society. Women's participation in society as described in the narratives presupposes a system in which women were able to maintain an elevated professional position into which were incorporated the roles of mother and educator. Just as significantly, these

women were in control of their own bodies and their own spiritual heritage.[98]

Moreover, Teubal believes that Sarah, as a symbol of women's struggle against subordination and oppression, is an ongoing source of support for contemporary women: "Over four thousand years later," she writes, "this same despair and this same struggle is being experienced by women in both social and religious spheres. But we are not alone. Sarah is there, standing on the threshold, waiting to be returned to her rightful place in history."[99]

Conclusion

During our time with Sarah, we have traveled to exotic places, seen her in a variety of situations—perilous, joyous, tragic—and viewed her from a broad spectrum of perspectives, both ancient and modern. Through the lenses of her various interpreters, Sarah has appeared as a goddess incarnate, a bitter shrew, a devoted mother, a prophetess greater than even Abraham himself. For many of these and a host of other readers, however, Sarah has often been a source of steadfastness and hope. Finding themselves "deep in the heart of Babylon, deep in the midst of exile," and casting about for a sustaining symbol, people throughout the ages have looked back to Sarah—full of years, great with child, great with hope, laughing at the impossibility of it all.

Notes

1. The singling out of Edom may reflect knowledge of specific, heinous offenses committed by Edomites against Jerusalem at the time of its destruction. (In addition to this text, see Obad. 1:12–15; Lam. 4:21–22). Relations between Edom and Judah were frequently strained, however, and the psalmist may simply employ Edom as a stereotypical antagonist. See Ackroyd, *Exile and Restoration,* p. 224. Judeans and Edomites remained hostile during the post-exilic period (see Isa. 34; Mal. 1:2–5).

2. King Jehoiachin was already in exile at the time of Jerusalem's destruction. He, along with other prominent Judeans, was deported in 597 B.C.E. as part of Babylon's attempt to prevent further Judean rebellions.

3. *Tanakh* has "who brought you forth."

4. In the book of Genesis, the names "Abram" and "Sarai" are used from 11:26 through 17:5 (when Abram's name is changed to Abraham) and 17:15 (when Sarai's name is changed to Sarah). As I tell their story, I shall conform to this biblical practice. Certain ancient commentators used "Abraham" and "Sarah" in their remarks about events that transpired *prior* to the name changes, however; I have simply quoted them, despite the inconsistency.

5. According to Gen. 17:25, Ishmael was thirteen years old when he was circumcised. At that point, Isaac had not yet been conceived. Ishmael and his mother were not expelled, however, until after Isaac was weaned (21:8), probably at age two or three.

6. Many scholars believe that the "Elohistic" or "E" source was composed in Northern Israel about 850 B.C.E.

7. The Priestly writers probably should be placed in the late exilic and early post-exilic period, from 550–450 B.C.E.

8. Presumably, YHWH is addressing the semidivine beings who are members of the divine council (see also Isa. 6:1–7; Job 1:6–12).

9. Hebrew *bālal;* hence, the wordplay on "Babel" (i.e., "Babylon").

10. Brueggemann, *Genesis,* p. 105.

11. Or, "be blessed."

12. Genesis (Lech Lecha) XLV 4, p. 381. In the Bible, only Hannah, the mother of Samuel, actually prays to be relieved of her barrenness (1 Sam. 1:10–11). According to the rabbis, however, the fact that Hannah prayed was sufficient evidence that all of the other barren women prayed as well. See Callaway, *Sing, O Barren One,* pp. 123–130.

13. Genesis (Lech Lecha) XLV 4, p. 382.

14. Von Rad, *Genesis,* p. 164.

15. Ginzberg, *The Legends of the Jews,* vol. 1, p. 221.

16. *Baba Bathra 16a,* p. 80.

17. Obviously a container, but not one intended for a corpse.

18. For the author of this legend, pepper was a costly spice.

19. Ginzberg, *Legends,* pp. 221–222; see also Genesis (Lech Lecha) XL 5, p. 329.

20. Ginzberg, *Legends,* p. 222.

21. Ibid., pp. 222–223.

22. Unlike Gen. 20:1–18, where Sarah is jeopardized by King Abimelech of Gerar, our text does not explicitly state whether Pharaoh had sexual intercourse with Sarah or not. The rabbis insisted that Pharaoh failed in his advances to her, however, because Yahweh sent an angel, armed with a stick, who struck at him every time he approached her (Ginzberg, *Legends,* p. 224; see also Genesis [Lech Lecha] XLI 2, pp. 333–334).

23. The scene prefigures the plagues that will afflict Egypt prior to Israel's exodus from slavery.

24. Abram may mean either "exalted father" or "he is exalted with respect to father" (i.e., his is a distinguished family line). The meaning of Abraham is uncertain. The biblical explanation of its meaning ("father of a multitude" [of nations]) is a popular etymology lacking philological support. Perhaps Abraham is an expanded variant of Abram. See *The Interpreter's Dictionary of the Bible,* s.v. "Abraham," and *Encyclopaedia Judaica,* s.v. "Abraham."

25. Both Sarai and Sarah mean "princess." Nevertheless, the rabbis found significance in her change of name. Rabbi Mana believed that the meaning of the latter spelling was more comprehensive: "Formerly she was a princess [Sarai] to her own people only, whereas now she is a princess [Sarah] to all mankind" (Genesis [Lech Lecha] XLVII 1, pp. 399–400).

26. Chapter 18 is attributed to the Yahwist.

27. Although the Hebrew verb is the same in both passages, Speiser renders 17:17 as "Abraham threw himself on his face, and he smiled as he said to himself, 'Can a child be born to one who is 100 years old, and could Sarah give birth at 90?' " He chooses to render *yitzchāq* in this way because "the concept of Abraham in a derisive attitude toward God would be decidedly out of keeping with *P*'s character" (*Genesis,* p. 125). His translation of 18:12, "So Sarah laughed to herself, saying, 'Withered as I am, am I still to know enjoyment—and my husband so old!' " is followed by the comment that "there is nothing equivocal . . . where Sarah is concerned. She is depicted as down-to-earth to a fault, with her curiosity, her impulsiveness, and her feeble attempt at deception . . . her impetuous reaction was one of derision" (p. 131).

28. Ginzberg, *Legends,* p. 240.

29. The Hebrew Bible bears witness to ancient Israel's concern that hospitality—the provision of protection and sustenance—be extended to sojourners. (See, for example, Gen. 19:1–11, 24:14–61; Judg. 19:10–25.)

30. According to the rabbis, this "servant-boy" was actually Ishmael. Abraham was trying to teach him about hospitality (Genesis [Vayera] XLVIII 13, p. 414).

31. The Bible contains no story of a return visit by this "guest" in the following year.

32. Interestingly enough, it is their advanced years and Sarah's post-menopausal state, rather than her barrenness (a term that can be applied meaningfully only to a woman in her childbearing years), that is lifted up at this point. In the quotation that follows, Sarah cites the improbability that she and her aged husband will engage in sexual intercourse.

33. This question, which has launched many a sermon, won the praise of Gerhard von Rad, who wrote that it "reposes in the story like a precious stone in a priceless setting, and its significance surpasses the cozy patriarchal milieu of the narra-

tive; it is a heuristic witness to God's omnipotent saving will" (*Genesis,* p. 202). In one sense, it is a rhetorical query; its obvious answer is "no." In another sense, it is a genuine question that demands an answer. Was it just this question that drew the anonymous prophet of the exile (the so-called "Second Isaiah") to hold up Abraham and Sarah as models of hope? Did he wish to place it before his audience so that they, too, would be forced to confront and answer it for themselves?

34. *Genesis,* p. 202. See also n. 30 above. Von Rad notes that setting up a woman as a negative foil to a man was a favorite literary device (Ibid., p. 203).

35. Ibid., pp. 199–200.

36. Ginzberg, *Legends,* pp. 241–242; "Shekinah," a feminine noun, refers to the presence of God.

37. Ibid., p. 243.

38. Genesis (Vayera) XLVIII 14, pp. 414–415.

39. Ginzberg, *Legends,* p. 243.

40. Genesis (Vayera) XLVIII 16, p. 416; Ginzberg, *Legends,* pp. 243–244.

41. Ginzberg, *Legends,* p. 244.

42. Ibid., pp. 244–245.

43. Because Abraham did not, in Genesis 21, *ask* Sarah to say that she was his sister (compare 12:13 with 20:2), the rabbis concluded that Sarah did not give her consent to this second deception. She, unlike Abraham, had learned her lesson on the first occasion (Genesis [Vayera] LII 4, p. 453).

In "Ishmael and Hagar" (pp. 237–238), Elie Wiesel ponders the negative light cast upon Abraham's character as a result of the two endangered matriarch stories:

> We don't understand Abraham; was he fearful for his life? And what about his honor? How can he abandon his wife— his adored, beloved wife—to the whims of a king who has an eye for a woman's beauty, especially that of a stranger? How can a hero like Abraham, who has defeated five kings, yield to a single one without so much as a fight? How is it possible that a man of his stature thinks only of saving his own skin? Admittedly, he is preoccupied with theological questions, but is there nothing of the romantic in him, nothing of chivalry?

I am grateful that, prior to its publication, Professor Wiesel made available to me a copy of the galleys for "Ishmael and Hagar."

44. According to this view, the Elohistic account, like the Yahwist's story, was originally positioned immediately after Abram's response to God's initial promise that his innumerable offspring would inherit the land of Canaan (Gen. 12:1–9). It therefore posed a prompt threat to that promise.

45. For a careful analysis of the differences between the three endangered matriarch stories and an investigation of how those differences contribute to their canonical literary contexts, see Polzin, "The Ancestress of Israel in Danger," pp. 81–98.

46. In Gen. 12:10–20 (attributed to the Yahwist), we are not told how Pharaoh learned of Sarai's actual relationship to Abram. Dreams are, for the Elohist, a favored means of divine communication with human beings.

47. For the view that genuine prophets are effective intercessors, see Num. 12:13, 21:7; Deut. 9:26; 1 Sam. 12:19–23.

48. Was the information presupposed, suppressed, or unknown by the author of 11:26–32? Note that in 11:29, the name of the father of Milcah (wife of Nahor and a much less important character than Sarai) is provided.

49. Genesis (Vayera) LII 11, p. 457.

50. *Sanhedrin 58b*, p. 396.

51. We shall return to this question when we discuss recent treatments of the Sarah traditions by feminist scholars.

52. Ginzberg, *Legends*, p. 261.

53. According to the rabbis, Isaac was born on the first day of Passover (ibid.).

54. In *Midrash Rabbah*, the rabbis reflected upon the miracle that Sarah was able to nurse Isaac. For them, Sarah's milk was a manifestation of God's power. They wrote, "Our mother Sarah was extremely modest. Said Abraham to her: 'This is not a time for modesty, but uncover your breasts so that all may know that the Holy One, blessed be He, has begun to perform miracles.' She uncovered her breasts and the milk gushed forth as from two fountains, and noble ladies came and had their children suckled by her" (Genesis [Vayera] LIII 9, p. 468). According to Jewish legend, all righteous converts to Judaism are descendants of these non-Jewish children nursed by Sarah (Ginzberg, *Legends*, p. 263).

55. For Gerhard von Rad, these verses, with their emphasis upon the word "laugh," suggest that at an earlier stage in the tradition Sarah named Isaac (meaning "he laughs"); her statements both accompanied, and elucidated, her choice of name (*Genesis*, p. 226).

56. Ginzberg, *Legends*, pp. 261–262; see also Genesis (Vayera) LIII 8, p. 467.

57. Ginzberg, *Legends*, p. 262.

58. We shall explore the question of Sarah's guilt when we turn to feminist perspectives on Hagar's story in chapter four.

59. Among Jews, this story is called the *Akeda*.

60. Ginzberg, *Legends*, p. 280.

61. Ibid., pp. 285–286.

62. At the conclusion of Genesis 22, we learn that Milcah, Abraham's sister-in-law, had children, including Bethuel, the father of Rebekah, who would become Isaac's wife (vs. 22–23). *Midrash Rabbah* notes the significance of this juxtaposition, such that a reference to Rebekah precedes the announcement of Sarah's death: "Before the Holy One, blessed be He, allowed Sarah's sun to set, He caused that of Rebekah to rise" (Genesis [Chayye Sarah] LVIII 2, p. 510). Rabbi Obadiah ben Jacob Sforno, an Italian commentator (about 1475–1550), explained further: Rebekah's birth was mentioned prior to Sarah's death, because "one righteous person does not die before another is born" (quoted in Freedman, "The Book of Genesis," p. 118).

63. Ginzberg, *Legends*, pp. 274–276.

64. From this legend, which is heavily influenced by the rabbis' knowledge of Job 1:6–12, we learn that Satan was responsible for the binding of Isaac in Genesis 22. He suggested to God that Abraham was a faithful devotee of Yahweh only so long as he wanted something—a son. Now that he had Isaac, however, Abraham had stopped building altars and offering sacrifices. The Lord replied that Abraham would sacrifice Isaac if ordered to do so, and the famous test of faith began (Ginzberg, *Legends*, pp. 272–273).

65. Ibid., pp. 286–287.

66. Ibid., p. 287. According to another tradition, Abraham returned from Mount Moriah alone and Sarah, realizing that Satan had not lied to her, died of sorrow (Ibid., pp. 285–286).

67. Speiser, *Genesis*, p. 169. Speiser quotes a Nuzi adoption text that stipulates the adopted person's obligation to his father: "When A dies, B shall weep for him and bury him."

68. Ginzberg, *Legends*, pp. 287–288.

69. Ibid., p. 290.

70. Gen. 16:5.

71. Genesis (Lech Lecha) XLV 7, pp. 383–384.

72. Callaway, *Sing O Barren One*, p. 71. She adds that "for Second Isaiah one might almost say that this [new] creation [of Israel] was pre-figured in the birth of Isaac. The authoritative tradition becomes a valid "interpreter' of the present situation; hence Sarah is almost a 'type' for Jerusalem."

73. The Hebrew word for city, *'îr*, is a feminine noun. In the Hebrew Bible, cities are frequently personified as females.

74. See Callaway, *Sing, O Barren One*, pp. 117–123. As Callaway notes, the prophets believed that the transformation of Jerusalem would be accomplished on earth as part of Israel's history. The rabbis believed, however, that Jerusalem's restoration would be accomplished in the world to come. "While these concepts are by no means identical," she writes, "the same hermeneutical principle has been employed: the significance of the biblical stories is in their meaning for the future rather than the past" (p. 137).

75. Ibid., pp. 135–136.

76. Ibid., pp. 5–12.

77. Genesis (Lech Lecha) XXXIX 14, p. 324.

78. Callaway, *Sing, O Barren One*, pp. 123–130.

79. Genesis (Vayera) LIII 5, p. 465. This interpretation is, of course, a departure from the biblical emphasis upon the birth of Isaac as God's faithful fulfillment of the promise, rather than a reward for human righteousness.

80. Genesis (Lech Lecha) XLV 5, p. 383.

81. *Megillah 14a*, p. 82. The other prophetesses are Miriam, Deborah, Hannah, Abigail, Huldah, and Esther.

82. Ibid. According to the rabbis, Iscah ("the seer"), referred to in Gen. 11:29, was actually Sarah. See also Ginzberg, *Legends*, p. 203.

83. Nunnally-Cox, *Foremothers*.

84. Ibid., p. 9.

85. Ibid., p. 9.

86. Fuchs, "Literary Characterization of Mothers," pp. 117–136.

87. Following Adrienne Rich, Fuchs distinguishes between the social and legal institution of motherhood, and the personal and psychological dimension of motherhood.

88. Fuchs, "Literary Characterization of Mothers," p. 129.

89. It is important to remember that Fuchs is not asking a historical question ("What really happened to Abraham and Sarah on the day that the visitors appeared?"), but rather a literary question ("Why does the narrator present characters, events, and so on as he does?").

90. Fuchs, "Literary Characterization of Mothers," p. 129.

91. Ibid., p. 121.

92. Ibid., pp. 132–133.

93. Ibid., pp. 131–132.

94. Ibid., p. 118.

95. Sarah, Leah, and Rachel had matrilocal marriages, according to Teubal. Rebekah also expected such an arrangement but decided instead to go to Canaan and marry Isaac. In the biblical story, Abraham is quite insistent that his son not return to Mesopotamia (Gen. 24:6).

96. Teubal identifies an *en* as a Mesopotamian high priestess; a *naditu* was a Mesopotamian woman of high priestly rank, perhaps even of royal birth, who spent at least some time cloistered (pp. 25, 100 and passim). See also Oden, "Religious Identity and the Sacred Prostitution Accusation," in *The Bible without Theology,* pp. 147–152.

97. Teubal, *Sarah the Priestess,* p. 121.

98. Ibid., pp. 139–140.

99. Ibid., p. 140.

More than a Possession: Critical, Rabbinical, and Feminist Perspectives on Hagar

Who Was Hagar?

The stories of Ruth the Moabite and Hagar the Egyptian are similar in certain ways. Both young women were, from Israel's perspective, foreigners—the daughters of despised, enemy nations. Yet each left her homeland to dwell with Hebrews in the land of Canaan. Both were led by elderly women into sexual unions with older men; and in each case, the result was the birth of a son.

Despite such similarities, however, Hagar's story is really quite different from Ruth's. The latter woman was free to decide to follow her mother-in-law back to Bethlehem. Hagar, on the other hand, was Sarah's handmaiden, her property. She was not free to refuse her mistress' orders. The story of Ruth introduces us to characters whose behavior is exemplary. But we search in vain for an ideal character within the Hagar narratives. No one is blameless—not even God. In Ruth's story, Naomi's actions certainly are driven by her desire to relieve the barrenness of her family line. But the narrative suggests that she is also motivated by love and concern for her daughter-in-law. When Sarah acts to relieve the barrenness of her family line, however, she shows no such love or concern for Hagar. In fact, Sarah nowhere speaks directly to Hagar or even deigns to utter her name. She wishes to be "built up" through the children her servant will bear (Gen. 16:2), but Sarah regards Hagar herself as no more than a possession.

Hagar's story is filled with pain—so much pain that we may be tempted to forego it, to concentrate instead upon other, more comfortable narratives among the Abraham and Sarah traditions. Certainly, the rabbis recognized that the Hagar episodes were problematic. Early Jewish commentators were reluctant to admit that Abraham and Sarah were capable of cruelty. Their interpretations nevertheless included the view that the *Akeda,* the near sacrifice of Isaac (Genesis 22), was punishment for the injustice committed by Abraham and Sarah against an unloved son and his mother.

Like the rabbis, contemporary interpreters of scripture, including feminist and womanist scholars, wrestle with Hagar's troubling story. Their questions are sometimes startling, sometimes disturbing, but they often lead to new insights—different ways of thinking about an old, aching tradition.

Here, then, is Hagar's story. It is enriched by the scholarship of contemporary specialists, by the insights of rabbis, and by the interpretations of a diverse group of contemporary women. Read through their eyes and your own, then decide for yourself what you will do with Hagar and her son.

Sarah Uses Hagar

> How can Jewish history begin with a domestic quarrel
> between a rich elderly mistress and her young servant?
>   Elie Wiesel[1]

Genesis 16 begins with simple statements of fact: "Sarai,
Abram's wife, had borne him no children. She had an
Egyptian maidservant whose name was Hagar." Just one
chapter earlier, God had reiterated the promise to make
Abram's descendents a great nation; but Sarai is still barren, and she blames YHWH for her condition. She therefore decides to take the initiative and find her own
solution: "Look," she tells her husband, "the Lord has
kept me from bearing. Consort with my maid; perhaps I
shall be built up through her."[2] Sarai's proposal may strike
us as odious, but the text must be understood within its
own cultural context. Her suggestion was no bold initiative, but rather a resort to acceptable legal practice within
the ancient Near Eastern world. In his Genesis commentary, E. A. Speiser cites a Nuzi (east of the Tigris River)
document legislating a remarkably similar situation:

> If Gilimninu bears children, Shennima shall not take
> another wife. But if Gilimninu fails to bear children,
> Gilimninu shall get for Shennima a woman from the
> Lullu country (i.e., a slave girl) as concubine. In that
> case, Gilimninu herself shall have authority over the
> offspring.[3]

Moreover, Sarai's solution works. When master and
handmaiden cohabitate, Hagar conceives. The rabbis
claimed that she became pregnant after only a single inti-
macy, and they bemoaned Hagar's precipitate fertility in
the face of Sarai's endless barrenness. "Thorns are neither weeded nor sown," observed Rabbi Hanina ben
Pazzi, "yet of their own accord they grow and spring up,
whereas how much pain and toil is required before wheat
can be made to grow!"[4]

Who was Hagar? The Bible tells us little about her. In Genesis 16:1, we learn that she was an Egyptian and Sarai's *šipchâ,* her handmaiden. According to later Israelite law, Hagar's non-Israelite nationality was crucial, for while manumission was required for Hebrew slaves after a six-year term of service, non-Hebrew slaves remained a "perpetual possession."[5]

How did Hagar come to be Sarai's handmaiden? Was she sold into bondage by parents whose economic straits did not permit them to raise yet another child? Was she orphaned, forced to sell herself in order to survive? The Bible does not answer these questions. The rabbis filled in the gap, however, claiming that her servanthood was linked to Abram and Sarai's recent trip to Egypt (12:10–20). You will remember that Abram and his family journeyed down to Egypt in order to escape a famine in Canaan. As they were about to enter the land, Abram asked Sarai to say that she was his sister, lest the Egyptians kill Abram and take her for themselves. Sarai agreed, and Pharaoh added her to his harem. His household was stricken with plagues, however, and the hapless monarch returned Sarai to Abram with orders that the couple go—quickly! But before they left, the rabbis claimed, Pharaoh gave his daughter, Hagar, to Sarai as a gift. And how, you may ask, could a father reduce his own child, an Egyptian princess, to slavery? According to *Midrash Rabbah,* he acted in her best interest, for, he said, "Better let my daughter be a handmaid in this house than a mistress in another house."[6] Perhaps, the rabbis concluded, her royal blood accounted for Hagar's pride, defiance, and love of freedom.

Hagar's Response to Pregnancy

The Bible says that when Hagar realized she was pregnant, her mistress was "lowered in her eyes" (Gen. 16:4).

Translators have puzzled over the exact meaning of this phrase. The rabbis, motivated no doubt by a desire to exonerate Sarah as much as possible, explained it very much at Hagar's expense:

> No sooner had Hagar's union with Abraham been consummated, and she felt that she was with child, than she began to treat her former mistress contemptuously, though Sarah was particularly tender toward her in the state in which she was. When noble matrons came to see Sarah, she was in the habit of urging them to pay a visit to "poor Hagar," too. The dames would comply with her suggestion, but Hagar would use the opportunity to disparage Sarah. "My lady Sarah," she would say, "is not inwardly what she appears to be outwardly. She makes the impression of a righteous, pious woman, but she is not, for it she were, how could her childlessness be explained after so many years of marriage, while I become pregnant at once?"[7]

Some modern translators—for the same reason, perhaps—also render the phrase harshly. We read, for example, in the *New English Bible,* "When she knew she was with child, she despised her mistress." Phyllis Trible prefers the translation in *Tanakh:* "Her mistress was lowered in her esteem." In Trible's view, Hagar's pregnancy enabled her to perceive Sarah in a new way: the blinders of hierarchy vanished, and Hagar invited "mutuality and equality" between her mistress and herself. "Not hatred, but a reordering of the relationship [was] the point."[8]

Well, whether she was uppity or merely sought to initiate a new relationship with Sarai based on parity, Hagar's attitude elicited a swift response from her mistress. In anger, Sarah confronted her husband, saying: "The wrong done me is your fault! I myself put my maid in your bosom; now that she sees that she is pregnant, I am lowered in her esteem. The LORD decide between you and me!" (16:5).

Perhaps the narrator intends that we feel sorry for Abram at this moment. What has he done to deserve so vitriolic an attack? Sarai asked him to take her maidservant as a wife, so he did. Sarai wanted Hagar to become pregnant, and she did. Yet suddenly Abram is snagged between a tactless young woman and a contentious old shrew.[9]

Poor Abram—what should he do? He is caught in an impossible situation, for as we read in Prov. 30:21–23:

> [21]The earth shudders at three things,
> At four which it cannot bear:
> [22]A slave who becomes king;
> A scoundrel sated with food;
> [23]A loathsome woman who gets married;
> A slave-girl who supplants her mistress.

Perhaps he should reason with Sarai and show compassion toward Hagar, who is young and pregnant to boot. After all, Eli Wiesel notes, "Hagar is Sarah's victim and Sarah was wrong to impose a role upon her and then begrudge her for playing it too well."[10] But possibly Abram feels constrained to follow the legal practice of his day. After all, ancient Near Eastern law addressed such a dilemma. The Hammurabi Code, for example, penalized a slave who, after becoming her master's concubine, attempted to achieve equal status with the first wife. The particular law in question concerns the female slave of a married hierodule (priestess) and so may not fit Sarah's situation exactly.[11] The circumstances described, however, are a striking parallel:

> When a seignior married a hierodule and she gave a female slave to her husband and she has then borne children, if later that female slave has claimed equality with her mistress because she bore children, her mistress may not sell her; she may mark her with the slave-mark and count her among the slaves.[12]

What does Abram do? Does he show compassion for
Hagar and speak in her defense? Does he rebuke Sarai
for her strident tone? No, he follows legal custom and the
wishes of his number one wife. He abrogates relations
with Hagar, demoting her to her former slave status and
placing her fate under Sarai's control. "Your maid is in
your hands," he says. "Deal with her as you think right"
(Gen. 16:6). "Then," we read, "Sarai treated her harshly,
and she ran away from her."[13] The precise nature of this
severe treatment is not described in the text. *Midrash
Rabbah* includes the view that Sarai did not actually hurt
Hagar, but rather forced her again to do the work of a
slave—to carry water buckets and towels for baths.[14] But
the Hebrew verb, *'nh,* bears severe connotations. It is
used, for example, to describe the suffering endured by
the Israelites during their enslavement in Egypt.[15] "Ironi-
cally," Trible writes, "here it depicts the torture of a lone
Egyptian woman in Canaan, the land of her bondage to
the Hebrews."[16] With typical eloquence, Trible character-
izes Hagar's plight:

> In the hand of Sarai, with the consent of Abram, Ha-
> gar becomes the suffering servant, the precursor of
> Israel's plight under Pharaoh. Yet no deity comes to
> deliver her from bondage and oppression; nor does
> she beseech one. Instead, this tortured female claims
> her own exodus. "Sarai afflicted her, and so she fled
> (*brḥ*) from her"—even as Israel will later flee (*brḥ*) from
> Pharaoh (Exod. 14:5a).[17]

The Refugee Returns with a Promise

Preferring the desert's dangers to Sarah's revenge, Hagar heads southwest toward Egypt, her home. At an oasis
near Shur, however, she is stopped by a messenger of the
Lord.[18] For what purpose does she receive a divine visita-

tion? Has YHWH's emissary sought out Hagar—pregnant, physically abused, thrice oppressed as Egyptian, slave, and woman—in order to comfort her? A victim at Sarah's hand, will Hagar now receive solace from the hand of the Lord? "Hagar, slave of Sarai," the angel says, "where have you come from, and where are you going?" (Gen. 16:8). Trible notes the significance of this address:

> For the first time a character speaks to Hagar and uses her name. The deity acknowledges what Sarai and Abram have not: the personhood of this woman. Yet the appositive, "maid of Sarai," tempers the recognition, for Hagar remains a servant in the vocabulary of the divine.[19]

Hagar responds to the first part of the question: "I am running away from my mistress Sarai," she says (16:8). About her destination and her future, however, she says nothing. The next words are the angel's; and they are scarcely comforting to Hagar or comfortable to us, the readers. "Go back to your mistress," the messenger says, "and submit to her harsh treatment" (16:9). "Hagar must go back to Sarah," von Rad explains, because YHWH "will not condone the break of legal regulations."[20] But should we then conclude that YHWH sanctions abuse? Where is the God of the exodus, who liberates people from their oppressors? Where is Hagar's redeemer?

But then Hagar, too, receives a divine promise. In the very next verse, in language strikingly reminiscent of God's promise to Abram, the angel of YHWH proclaims, "I will greatly increase your offspring, and they shall be too many to count" (16:10b). Is the "patriarchal promise" actually being extended to a *woman*? Jo Ann Hackett notes how very surprising verse 10 really is: "This is the only case in Genesis where this typical J-writer promise is given to a woman rather than to a patriarch, and so we sit up and take notice."[21] Surely these words are intended to comfort Hagar. After all, a divine promise of numerous offspring is no small thing, even if it does not carry with it a concomitant pledge that those children will inherit *land* on which to live. Moreover, the promise is followed by a speech concerning her unborn child:

> [11]Behold, you are with child
> And shall bear a son;
> You shall call him Ishmael,[22]
> For the LORD has paid heed to your suffering.
> [12]He shall be a wild ass of a man;
> His hand against everyone,
> And everyone's hand against him;
> He shall dwell alongside of all his kinsmen
> (Gen. 16:11–12).[23]

Are these verses also intended to comfort Hagar? They do not speak to the physical suffering that she has endured, and will continue to endure, when she returns to her mistress. But in biblical narrative, mothers are generally characterized as being most concerned with their children's well-being, rather than their own;[24] perhaps from the narrative's perspective, these words about Ishmael, Hagar's future offspring, are indeed a panacea for her pain. Von Rad finds in verse 12 "a worthy son of his rebellious and proud mother! In this description of Ishmael there is undoubtedly undisguised sympathy and admiration for the roving Bedouin who bends his neck to no yoke."[25] The rabbis saw it differently, however, as Elie Wiesel notes:

> He would be wild. . . . He would have his fingers in everything. The commentators did not hesitate to explain: He would be a thief. Violent. Poor thing: He isn't even born yet and already he is being accused of crimes and sins as vague as they are unfair. He is not even born yet and already he is being made an antisocial being. From the moment he arrives, what does he

see? Helpless, he is witness to some painful scenes: His mother is humiliated without end. What must he think of the system in which he grows up? What must he think of the patriarch Abraham whose reputation transcends borders? Or of his God who permits so much injustice within His human family?[26]

Hagar's response to these divine disclosures is to name God—an astonishing act undertaken by no other person in the Hebrew Bible.[27] "You are El-roi ["God of seeing"]," she says (16:13), but the following explanation for her choice of name is lamentably unclear.[28] Walter Brueggemann is content to leave the text alone. "The disclosure was not greatly valued in the tradition," he notes, "and is best left in its obscurity."[29] Trible cannot resolve the textual difficulties either, but she very much wishes to value Hagar's initiative and insight:

The maid who, after seeing (*r'h*) her conception of a child, had a new vision of her mistress Sarai (16:4), now, after receiving a divine announcement of the forthcoming birth, sees (*r'h*) God with new vision. Hagar is a theologian. Her naming unites the divine and human encounter: the God who sees and the God who is seen.[30]

Following her experience with the apparition, Hagar goes back. What were her thoughts during the long journey home, a journey *away* from her home? Did she question whether the angel was real, or just a mirage? Did she kick herself each step of the way? Would she later regret her decision to fall in with God's plan? The narrative neither asks nor answers these questions. Nevertheless, this scene ends on a painful note that even the birth of baby Ishmael cannot relieve; over the blessed event hangs the divine messenger's prediction: "His hand against everyone, and everyone's hand against him" (16:2).

The Expulsion of Hagar and Ishmael

Years later, the Lord again appears to Abram, changing his name to Abraham and reiterating the promise that Sarah will bear a son. Abraham falls on his face and laughs (Gen. 17:17). Later, he hosts a meal for three visitors; and one of them repeats the pledge that Sarah will become pregnant. *She* laughs. But then Sarah conceives. Sarah conceives? Oh, yes! God gets the last laugh. Sarah gives birth to Isaac, a name meaning "he laughs." The child survives the perilous years of infancy and is weaned. To celebrate, Abraham hosts an enormous feast.

Then, the text says, "Sarah saw the son whom Hagar the Egyptian had borne to Abraham *mĕtzachēq*."[31] She said to Abraham, 'Cast out that slave-woman and her son, for the son of that slave shall not share in the inheritance with my son Isaac' " (21:9–10). Do you hear the derision in Sarah's voice? She does not stoop to call these people by name. She does not even refer to Hagar as her maid-servant. No, Hagar is "that slave-woman."

What did Ishmael do, that Sarah should treat them in such fashion? The participle *mĕtzachēq* is a form of *tzchq,* the same Hebrew root underlying Isaac's name (*Yitzchāq*). But surely Sarah was not angry because Ishmael was simply laughing, having fun with Isaac. Maybe so, says von Rad. She may well have been angry for just that reason: "What Ishmael did need not be anything evil at all. The picture of the two boys playing with each other on an equal footing is quite sufficient to bring the jealous mother to a firm conclusion: Ishmael must go!"[32] The rabbis sought greater justification for Sarah's actions, however. They insisted that, in this context, *mĕtzachēq* meant something dreadful, indeed. *Midrash Rabbah,* for example, records a variety of meanings for the word. In the following excerpt, the rabbis are determining the gist of the word in other passages of scripture where it appears and then transferring those connotations to the present context to illumine its meaning:

R. Simeon b. Yohai said: R. Akiba used to interpret this to his [Ishmael's] shame. Thus R. Akiba lectured: AND SARAH SAW THE SON OF HAGAR THE EGYPTIAN, WHOM SHE HAD BORNE UNTO ABRAHAM, MAKING SPORT. Now MAKING SPORT refers to nought else but immorality, as in the verse, *The Hebrew servant, whom thou hast brought unto us, came in unto me to make* sport *of me* (Gen. xxxix, 17).[33] Thus this teaches that Sarah saw Ishmael ravish maidens, seduce married women and dishonour them. R. Ishmael taught: This term SPORT refers to idolatry, as in the verse, *And rose up to* make sport (Ex. xxxii, 6).[34] This teaches that Sarah saw Ishmael build altars, catch locusts, and sacrifice them. R. Eleazar said: The term sport refers to bloodshed, as in the verse, *Let the young men, I pray thee, arise and* sport *before us* (II Sam. II, 14).[35] R. 'Azariah said in R. Levi's name: Ishmael said to Isaac, "Let us go and see our portions in the field"; then Ishmael would take a bow and arrows and shoot them in Isaac's direction, whilst pretending to be playing. Thus it is written, *As a madman who casteth firebrands, arrows, and death; so is the man that deceiveth his neighbour, and saith: Am not I in sport* (Prov. xxii, 18f.)? But I say:[36] This term sport [mockery] refers to inheritance. For when our father Isaac was born all rejoiced, whereupon Ishmael said to them, "You are fools, for I am the firstborn and I receive a double portion."[37]

In Genesis 16, Abram agreed to Sarai's request that he sleep with Hagar. He is distressed, however, by her demand that Hagar and Ishmael be expelled. Poor Abraham—how can Sarah be so heartless? Do the actions of a child justify throwing both his firstborn son and the boy's mother out of their home, the only security they know? In his commentary, Brueggemann writes: "The story knows what it wants to tell. Isaac is the child of the future. But the story has no easy time imposing its will on the characters. Ishmael will not be so easily reduced. He has some claims. He has a claim because he is the oldest son of father Abraham. He is not adopted, not an intruder, but born to the man of promise."[38] Abraham resists. But then God says to him, "Do not be distressed over the boy or your slave; whatever Sarah tells you, do as she says, for it is through Isaac that offspring shall be continued for you. As for the son of the slave-woman, I will make a nation of him, too, for he is your seed" (21:12–13).

Early next morning, Abraham prepares bread and a skin of water for Hagar and Ishmael to take on their journey. But why, the rabbis asked, did he insist that they leave early in the morning? "For two reasons," Elie Wiesel writes.

> First: he wanted Hagar and her son to set out before sunrise, before the great heat—when it is still possible to walk on the sand. Second: Abraham wanted to say farewell to his son and the boy's mother without Sarah being present. Sarah was still asleep. This was the right moment to see his son off. What if he were to get too emotional? If he were to burst into tears? Worse: what if Sarah were to look for a quarrel and say that he was giving them too much bread, too much water? No, it is better that she is not there.[39]

According to verse 14, Abraham places Ishmael, as well as food and water, on Hagar's shoulder. But this statement, we have noted, creates a problem for readers. How can Ishmael, who was Abraham's only son when he was circumcised at thirteen years of age (17:25), and who now has a brother old enough to be weaned, possibly be carried by his mother?

According to the rabbis, Sarah threw Ishmael an evil glance, making him so ill and feverish that his mother had to carry him, despite his size.[40] Modern biblical scholars have understood the problem differently, however. They find considerable evidence within the Abraham and

Sarah traditions that episodes, many of which were first transmitted as oral traditions, only gradually came to be linked together in various written sources. It was the Priestly writers, the last to rework the material, who added the account of male circumcision within Abraham's household when Ishmael was thirteen years old (17:23–27). That datum forces the reader of the traditions in their final, canonical form to ascribe to Ishmael a more advanced age than is appropriate to the details of the expulsion episode in verses 14–16.

Homeless, helpless, Hagar wanders in the wilderness of Beer-sheba. Gone is the defiant woman who fled from her abusive mistress and moved with certainty through the desert.[41] The Hebrew verb used to describe her action in verse 14 (*t'h*) conveys a sense of uncertainty and loss of direction.[42] Soon, their water is gone, and her son begins to suffer. And so, the text says, "[Hagar] left the child under one of the bushes, and went and sat down at a distance a bowshot away, for she thought, 'Let me not look on as the child dies.'[43] And sitting thus afar, she burst into tears" (21:15–16). Who can read these words and fail to ache for Hagar and Ishmael?

Hagar and Ishmael Are Rescued

Does Hagar cry out to God? Does she beseech YHWH to save her son's life? Would you? Would you appeal to the God who had ordered you back to bondage and beatings? Would you entreat the God who sanctioned your mistress's plan to expel you and your child, not so that you might be freed from slavery, but rather to safeguard the future of your oppressors?[44] Would you implore such a God? Hagar does not. She weeps, but not to YHWH. And the Lord, it seems, does not respond to Hagar's grief. Although the Hebrew text plainly states that "she burst into tears," the following sentence reads "God heard the cry *of the boy*" (emphasis added). Many modern commentators, following the Septuagint, emend the text so that this inconsistency is removed. Von Rad, for example, renders the end of verse 16 "And as she sat over against him, the child lifted up his voice and wept."[45] The rabbis explained it differently, claiming that God responded to Ishmael because Hagar was praying to idols, while the boy's words were directed to YHWH: "O Lord of the world!" he cried, "If it be Thy will that I shall perish, then let me die in some other way, not by thirst, for the tortures of thirst are great beyond all others."[46] Trible believes that the shift from Hagar's tears to God's regard for the lad reflects patriarchal preoccupation with the fate of men and their male offspring. Hagar may be the focus of verses 14b–16, but she is not the narrative's principle interest. From verse 17 on, "concern for the male deflects interest from the female."[47] However, Elsa Tamez, a Latin American liberation theologian, regards Ishmael's name as a clue to the reason for shifting from Hagar to her son: "God has heard the cry of Ishmael; he is called Ishmael, because God is, and always will be, ready to hear the cries of the son of a slave. Ishmael signifies in Hebrew 'God hears,' and God will always listen to children such as Ishmael who are the victims of injustice."[48]

For a second time, Hagar is questioned by an angel of the Lord: "What troubles you, Hagar?" (21:17) he asks from heaven. Before she can speak, however, the messenger continues: "Fear not, for God has heeded the cry of the boy where he is. Come, lift up the boy and hold him by the hand, for I will make a great nation of him" (21:17–18). YHWH opens Hagar's eyes, and suddenly she spies a well. She fills the skin with water and gives her son a drink.[49] In the years that follow, Ishmael lives in the desert and becomes a skilled archer.[50] His mother arranges his marriage to an Egyptian woman.[51] And, the text says, "God was with *the boy* (Gen. 21:20, emphasis added).

But what of Hagar, the rabbis wondered. Did she live a long life? Did she ever find happiness with a man who loved and honored her for herself? Yes, they replied, pointing to the biblical tradition that, after Sarah's death, Abraham married a woman named Keturah who bore him six sons (25:1). Who was this Keturah? Rabbi Judah identified her: She was Hagar.[52] Throughout the years of their separation, Hagar had never remarried.[53] Now she and Abraham were together again.

The Bible does not tell us these things, however. Hagar's name appears once more, in the genealogical list of Genesis 25:12. But she does not reappear in a biblical narrative (although Paul refers to her in Gal. 4:21–31). In the Bible, Hagar might be regarded as a "throw-away" character,[54] for she is not part of Israel's salvation history. On the contrary, Hagar and Ishmael are depicted as a *threat* to the fulfillment of God's promise to Abraham and Sarah. But Hagar must not be thrown away. We must affirm what Abraham and Sarah do not: Hagar is more than a possession; she is a human being.

Indeed, recent interpreters discern biblical evidence that Hagar was quite an important person. When she fled from Sarai's beatings, a divine messenger found her at the spring near Shur. Hagar is the first person in the Bible to be visited by a heavenly messenger.[55] She is the only woman to receive a promise of innumerable descendants from God and the only individual in scripture to name God. Have we misjudged the biblical message? Perhaps, as Tamez suggests, these narratives are included in the canon precisely to show that "the oppressed are also God's children, co-creators of history. God does not leave them to perish in the desert without leaving a trace." On the contrary, "they must live to be part of history, and struggle to be subjects of it."[56]

The stories of Abraham and Sarah are filled with promise and hope. Through these, our ancient ancestors in the faith, YHWH acted to bring about a great history of salvation. Hagar's story reminds us, however, that one person's salvation history can be another person's history of oppression.

Who Is to Blame? A Modern Midrashic Perspective

Who is responsible for this tragedy? Who caused so much pain within the household God chose to be a blessing to the nations? In "Ishmael and Hagar," Elie Wiesel poses just this question; and it is not easily answered, because each character has both strengths and weaknesses, assets and flaws. Each character is, in short, human. Well, not everyone is human. God, too, has a role to play in Hagar's story; and God, too, must be confronted by the question of blame. "Where does this tragedy begin?" Wiesel asks. "When does the conflict begin? . . . Does the conflict begin when God made too many promises to too many people at the same time?" And again,

> Why did He prevent Sarah from conceiving? And why did He advise—no, command—Abraham to obey his wife and banish Hagar and her child? God could have abstained. He did not have to be directly involved in this business. In fact, Abraham and Sarah could have put the whole blame on Him! It is His fault, and the human beings could do nothing! . . . If Abraham and Sarah had committed an injustice toward Hagar and Ishmael, it is because they were caught in a situation willed and ordered by God.[57]

But surely we cannot simply exonerate human beings at God's expense. And so Wiesel must consider each of the other characters in this story—all but Isaac, that is, for he really was too young to blame. Does young Ishmael also escape the onus of responsibility? We cannot say with certainty, Wiesel concludes. True, he is young and a victim, as Genesis 21:15–19 make all too clear. Nevertheless, the rabbis questioned his behavior toward Isaac, and the *mĕtzachēq* of 21:9 is too suggestive, too mysterious, to disregard completely.

What of Hagar? Is she blameless, the victim of Sarah's hostility and Abraham's indifference? Oh no, says Wiesel. The Code of Hammurabi alone indicts her. "On a purely anthropological level, she is guilty," he writes. "She got only what she deserved. She had only to respect the rules of the game. Arrogance must get its due, and social transgressions must be punished."[58] Moreover, when she and Ishmael are in the desert, and the child becomes ill, she casts him under a bush and leaves him there. Is this any way for a mother to behave? "Surely, she loves him and cannot bear his illness or his slow and cruel agony. But why doesn't she think of *him*, of *his* needs? Doesn't Ishmael need her?"[59] But perhaps, Wiesel later suggests, we have judged Hagar too harshly. "She distances herself so she can cry out loud. As long as she is near her son, she manages to hold back her tears—so as not to frighten him, not to distress him. What could be more natural, more human, on the part of a mother?"[60] No, we should not blame Hagar. Perhaps she did become a bit haughty after she discovered her pregnancy; still, a little arrogance scarcely justifies the abuse, rejection, and desolation she endured. Like Ishmael, Hagar is a victim in this story, not a villian.

Is it Abraham, then? Is he to blame for the pain and strife that have torn his family apart? As we shall see, the biblical narrator goes to great lengths to exculpate him. According to the text, it was Sarai, and not her husband, who abused Hagar. She, not he, devised the plan to expel her rivals forever. Moreover, Abraham resisted her demands until God intervened directly, demanding his assent. But perhaps, Wiesel suggests, Abraham's sin was precisely his failure to take a more active role in events: "Did Sarah hate him [Ishmael]? What a pity. Abraham should have explained the situation to her. Did God side with Sarah? What a pity. Abraham should have argued with him as he had done for Sodom."[61]

Some rabbis concluded that Abraham's treatment of Hagar and Ishmael was unjust. They pointed back to the time when Abram traveled to Egypt and asked Sarai to deceive Pharaoh. The pair had pretended to be siblings; because of their charade, innocent Egyptians were stricken with plagues. What was Abraham and Sarah's punishment for lying? "The tragedy of Hagar and Ishmael," Wiesel replies. "Had they not lied, the king would not have offered his daughter to Sarai. And the history of the Jews—and of Islam—would have been different."[62]

And yes, the *Akeda,* the near sacrifice of Isaac recorded in Genesis 22, also was regarded as punishment for Hagar and Ishmael's fate. "Here again," says Wiesel, "we find a Midrashic text that says Abraham was wrong when he preferred Isaac to Ishmael: no father has the right to favor one child over another."[63]

> Thus, when God orders Abraham to take Isaac and bring him to Mount Moriah, the sentence reads: *Kakh na et binkha et yehidkha asher ahavta et Itzhak.* "Take your son, your only son, the one you have loved, Isaac." But that is wrong! Isaac is not his only son! The punctuation needs to be changed. The sentence should read as follows: *Kakh na et binkha,* comma,—"Take your son"—*et yehidkha asher ahavta*—"the only one you have loved," comma, "Isaac." Thus the command contains a reproach as well as an explanation.[64]

But surely Abraham does not bear total responsibility for these events. What about Sarah—isn't she the worst offender of all? Are not her actions—the angry outbursts

at her husband, the physical abuse of pregnant Hagar,
the demand that a hapless mother and child be exposed
to the desert's dangers—self-centered and pitiless? In the
end, Wiesel sadly concludes that "the so-called villain in
this story is Sarah, our beautiful and noble grandmother
. . . . Of course she desired a glorious future for her son!
But she was wrong to do so at the expense of another
mother and another son." Wiesel's judgment finds support within his tradition:

> The great Rabbi Moshe ben Nahman—the Ramban—
> Nahmanides—comments that when our ancestress
> Sarai (or Sarah) persecuted Hagar, she committed a
> sin. Abraham, by not preventing her, became an ac-
> complice to that sin. That is why God heard the lament
> and the tears of Hagar and gave her a wild son whose
> descendants would torment in every way the descen-
> dants of Abraham and Sarah. The sufferings of the
> Jewish people, said the Ramban, derive from those
> which Sarah inflicted on Hagar.[65]

"Of course," Wiesel admits, "one could invent—or
formulate—all kinds of excuses to whitewash our grandmother. We have mentioned a few . . . . But apologies no
longer have a place in our tradition. We are sufficiently
mature to admit our shortcomings—especially since the
Torah itself chooses not to conceal them."[66] Israel's ancestors were human beings, and for that reason, Wiesel
claims, we love them all the more. Nevertheless, the story
of Ishmael and Hagar is an abiding source of sorrow. "If
only Sarah could have shared her love between Isaac and
Ishmael!" Wiesel laments. "If only she could have
brought them together instead of setting them apart!
Maybe some of today's tragedies would have been
avoided. The Palestinian problem is rooted in the separation of these two brothers. As always, we must ask, Is it
the mother's fault?"[67]

Who Is to Blame? Feminist Perspectives on Hagar and Her Story

I have quoted at length from Wiesel's study of the Hagar episodes, not only because it is a profound and deeply moving essay, but also because of his decision that when all is said and done, Sarah bears the greatest portion of guilt. Wiesel is by no means the only contemporary interpreter of Israel's traditions to draw this conclusion. To be sure, Tamez claims that "on reading the stories of Sarah and Hagar . . . we generally identify ourselves with Sarah, the beautiful wife of the great patriarch Abraham, the father of the faith."[68] And it is true that some modern scholars continue the early rabbinical practice of exonerating Sarah by emphasizing Hagar's insubordination and Ishmael's misconduct. Nevertheless, a number of contemporary women interpreters, while acknowledging that Sarah is herself a subordinate within her patriarchal culture, criticize her merciless treatment of Hagar and her son.[69]

In her sensitive essay "A Mistress, A Maid, and No Mercy," Renita Weems probes the tension separating Sarah and Hagar, both as part of an ancient story and as an all-too-contemporary, tragic reality.[70] Hagar is an African; Sarah is a Hebrew. But Weems insists that "it would not be totally fair to make the Old Testament story of Hagar and Sarai carry all the weight of the history of race relationships in the modern world."[71] Although mindful of the ethnic differences that separate these two women, Weems is more interested in how economic prejudice and sexual exploitation tear apart two covictims in a patriarchal society:

> The differences between the two women . . . went beyond their ethnic identities, beyond their reproductive

capabilities. Their disparities were centered in their contrasting economic positions. And economic differences have, on more than one occasion, thwarted coalitions and frustrated friendships between women.[72]

Sarai's womb was empty. Hagar (and her womb) belonged to her. So Sarai resolved to procure children through Hagar. With pregnancy, the maidservant conceived a new sense of self-worth. But her fresh self-perception angered her mistress, and Sarai beat her, badly enough that Hagar decided to run away:

> Taking advantage of Hagar's slavewoman status, exploiting the fact that the woman who tended to her house was vocationally limited and her financial options virtually non-existent, Sarai took advantage of her status over Hagar. She knew that the way to enslave a slave—all over again—was to humiliate her, to destroy her (new found) sense of self-worth, to dehumanize her.[73]

Perhaps in the long run, Weems suggests, it was best for Hagar and Ishmael that they leave Abraham's tent. "Sometimes we need a shove," she says, "—even from our enemies—to make us stand on our two feet." But that possibility cannot ameliorate the cruelty of Sarah's shove. "God had shown mercy to Sarah by granting her a child from her own womb. But Sarah was not willing, in turn, to show mercy to a woman whose back was up against the wall."[74]

Trible, too, holds Sarah primarily responsible for our tragic story. While she does not absolve Abraham of guilt, her focus nevertheless remains fixed upon the rivalry between Sarah and Hagar—an unfair fight, she insists, because Sarah is a wealthy, free Hebrew while Hagar is alone, poor, and a bonded alien. Hagar's story is terrifying because the narrator, although disapproving of Sarah's actions, nevertheless insists throughout the story

that YHWH backs Sarah.[75] Moreover, this ancient tale
speaks all too frighteningly of the present day. In our
own time, classism, ageism, sexism, racism, and national-
ism pit us against each other. Rich and powerful members of society ignore, exploit, and alienate the poor and
helpless in our midst. Like Sarah, they (we?) try to erase
from our "salvation history" the Hagars in our midst.[76]

The interpretations of both Weems and Trible are powerful; and I do not wish to detract from them. Neither do
I seek to exonerate Sarah as she appears in Genesis 16
and 21, for it is clear that she is responsible for a great
deal of suffering. Sarah does, indeed, wield power over
her maidservant; and, in her exercise of that power, she
abuses both Hagar and Ishmael. But are there limits to
her power? Both Weems and Trible know that there are:
Sarah uses power and maintains authority within the limits of patriarchal social structures.[77] Patriarchal society is
the stage upon which our story is played out. And, if we
may extend our metaphor a bit, both Sarah and Hagar
are actors under the direction—indeed, the total control—of a director: the anonymous, omniscient biblical
narrator. Is it possible that this narrator, by emphasizing
Sarah's culpability, seeks in the interest of patriarchy both
to separate these women from each other (and from his
readers) and to protect Abraham from criticism? Is Fuchs
correct when she insists that this story, by virtue of the
way it is told in Genesis 16 and 21, predisposes us to
certain attitudes about Sarah, Hagar, and Abraham?

Let us return to the text and look at it through Fuchs'
eyes. Sarah's first words in Genesis 16 are "Look, the
LORD has kept me from bearing" (16:2). Here, she expresses the ancient Israelite belief that YHWH controls the
wombs of women. Sarah lived for decades believing that
God had withheld children from her. The onus of barrenness was constantly upon her.[78] Despite her social status,
she bore a reproach. For what great sin is Sarah being
punished? her neighbors wondered and whispered about
her.

At length, Sarah felt compelled to place her maidservant in her husband's bed. From now on, she and Hagar would inevitably be competitors for Abraham's attention and approval. And they would have to learn to survive within the tensions of patriarchal polygyny—an institution that places more than one wife under the authority of a single husband.[79]

Now just as the biblical narrator does not question the misery caused by institutionalized slavery, neither does he ask whether patriarchal institutions are likely to cause women pain. On the contrary, the narrator "blames woman, the victim of patriarchy, for its pitfalls and shortcomings."[80] He suggests, for example, that if females suffer in polygynous relationships, it is not because such relationships are likely to be oppressive, but rather because women are vicious and competitive:

> By pitting against each other two women across lines of class, age, reproductive capability, and nationality, the Hagar stories are foregrounding women's rivalry as the "real" cause of their misery. Hidden in the background of the power struggle between these women [however] is the male protagonist for whose approval both women are vying. In this manner biblical ideology shifts our attention away from the source of the problem to its symptoms, blaming . . . the female victims of polygyny for its unsavory aspects.[81]

Protective of the patriarch's image, the narrative explicitly states that Hagar is back under Sarah's control when the physical abuse occurs. Moreover, it is no accident that Sarah, and not her husband, wants to expel "that slave women and her son." Abraham is depicted as unwilling to comply until YHWH explicitly commands that he do so. And, in his preparations for their departure, he exhibits the tenderness and concern that Sarah utterly lacks.[82] "Nowhere does the text allude to the father-husband's possible role in the antagonistic relationship of his cowives. Rather, he is portrayed as either obedient and understanding, or justly outraged but helpless to change anything."[83] Hence, Fuchs concludes, the biblical narrator deals with the strife in Abraham's house by exonerating both the patriarch and institutionalized polygyny, and by blaming women's nature, particularly as it is exhibited in Sarah. To the extent that our own interpretations highlight the conflict between mistress and handmaiden, we further the patriarchal objectives of the narrator.[84]

We are probably not going to get very far if we are content simply to blame the anonymous Israelite author for structuring his story according to the ideology of his day. After all, we are all products of our time to a significant degree, and we reflect our cultures to some extent both in the stories we tell and in the ways we tell them. Fuchs' work reminds us, however, that we are responsible for discerning those narrative techniques which predispose us to certain interpretations and conclusions. Only as we recognize such strategies can we make responsible decisions about whether we wish to fall in with them or not. I recognize, for example, that slavery is an integral part of this narrative. When I encounter slavery in the Bible, however, I understand it to be *descriptive* of circumstances in the ancient narrator's day, rather than *prescriptive* of conditions that God sanctions and that should, consequently, pertain in my own time. Likewise, I do not sanction patriarchy and the suffering it inflicts upon women simply because I encounter it within certain biblical texts.

Conclusion

Hagar's story haunts us because it is filled with so much pain and suffering. Did she find happiness one day, as the rabbis claimed? We can only hope so—if not with

Abraham, then in some other way. The Bible does not tell us her fate. It does, however, provide another glimpse of her son, Ishmael. Many years have passed. Abraham—God's chosen man, the Lord's instrument for blessing in a post-Babel world torn by sin and alienation—dies at the ripe old age of one hundred and seventy-five years. And both of his sons, Isaac and Ishmael, bury him in the cave of Machpelah, Sarah's final resting place. Are Isaac and Ishmael together again? Yes, says Wiesel, "Isaac *and* Ishmael were both there for the funeral. They were together, reconciled for this one event . . . the reunion of the two brothers before their father's grave . . . reminds us of a truth too many generations have tended to forget: both Isaac and Ishmael are Abraham's sons."[85]

The rabbis taught that of the seventy nations the Holy One has made only two, Isra*el* and Ishma*el*, bear God's name.[86] And in the Midrash, they foretold that, at the end of time, the Jewish sons of Israel and the Muslim sons of Ishmael will do battle in the Holy Land and destroy its cities.[87] Let us hope, however, that the rabbis were wrong, and the battles will not continue until the end of days. God grant that in the near future the children of Sarah and the children of Hagar are able to live together peacefully in the land promised to their father, Abraham.

Notes

1. Wiesel, "Ishmael and Hagar," p. 236. I had access to this article prior to its publication, because Professor Wiesel graciously provided me with a copy of the galleys.

2. *Tanakh* has "perhaps I shall have a son through her," noting that in Hebrew, "be built up" (from *bānâ*, "build up") is a play on *bēn* ("son").

3. Speiser, *Genesis*, p. 120.

4. Genesis (Lech Lecha) XLV 4, p. 381. The remark, of course, disparages both Ishmael and his offspring.

5. See Exod. 21:2–4; Deut. 15:12; Lev. 25:44–46, and *The Interpreter's Dictionary of the Bible*, s.v. "Slavery in the OT." According to Exod. 21:26–27, however, any slave who had been maimed by the owner could go free.

6. Genesis (Lech Lecha) XLV 1, p. 380.

7. Ginzberg, *The Legends of the Jews*, p. 238. See also Genesis (Lech Lecha) XLV 4, p. 382.

8. Trible, *Texts of Terror*, p. 12.

9. Fuchs, "A Jewish Feminist Reading of the Hagar Stories," p. 4. I am grateful to Professor Fuchs for making available to me a copy of this unpublished manuscript.

10. Wiesel, "Ishmael and Hagar," p. 238.

11. See, however, the discussion of Teubal's *Sarah the Priestess* in chapter three. Teubal claims that Sarah was, in fact, a priestess whose marriage to Abraham, her half-sibling, did not include sexual relations.

12. The law code of Hammurabi, a Babylonian king who ruled from about 1728 to 1686 B.C.E., is translated by Theophile J. Meek in *Ancient Near Eastern Texts*, ed. by Pritchard, p. 172.

13. In "Rehabilitating Hagar" (pp. 12–27), Hackett notes

similarities between the basic plot of Hagar's story in Genesis 16 (and Gen. 21:9–21), the Mesopotamian Gilgamesh epic, and the story of Aqhat from Ugarit.

14. Genesis (Lech Lecha) XLV 6, p. 384.

15. Trible, *Texts of Terror,* p. 13.

16. Ibid.

17. Ibid.

18. "Shur" probably refers to the frontier wall that was Egypt's northeastern boundary. See von Rad, *Genesis,* p. 187 (and also *Midrash Rabbah* XLV 7, p. 385, n. 1).

19. Trible, *Texts of Terror,* p. 15.

20. Von Rad, *Genesis,* p. 189.

21. Hackett, "Rehabilitating Hagar," p. 15. The "J-writer" to whom Hackett refers is the Yahwist, the tenth-century B.C.E. author-editor who compiled many of Israel's ancestral traditions.

22. I.e., "God heeds."

23. At this point, commentators frequently pause to discuss annunciation speeches—divine disclosures to a man and/or woman that they will have a son. (The Bible contains no annunciation speeches about the birth of a daughter.) Technically, the angel's address to Hagar is not an annunciation speech, because Hagar already knows that she is pregnant (v. 4). The rabbis believed, however, that the angel's words *were* a true annunciation speech, for they claimed that Hagar's first conception ended in miscarriage before her escape, when her jealous mistress "cast an evil eye upon her" (Ginzberg, *Legends,* p. 239). Ishmael, about whom the angel spoke, was not conceived until after Hagar returned to Sarai and Abram (so Rashi, quoted in *The Soncino Chumash,* p. 77).

24. Fuchs, "Literary Characterization of Mothers," pp. 132–133.

25. Von Rad, *Genesis,* p. 189.

26. Wiesel, "Ishmael and Hagar," p. 240.

27. Trible, *Texts of Terror,* pp. 17–18.

28. Von Rad (*Genesis,* p. 185) understands v. 13b to mean, "Have I really seen God and remained alive after seeing him?" Speiser (*Genesis,* p. 117) translates, "Did I not go on seeing here after he had seen me?" Booij renders the words, "Would I have gone here indeed looking for him that looks after me?" ("Hagar's Words in Genesis 16:1–13b," pp. 1–7). Trible (*Texts*

of Terror, p. 18) understands it to mean, "Have I even here seen (*r'h*) after the one who sees (*r'h*) me?"

29. Brueggemann, *Genesis,* p. 153.

30. Trible, *Texts of Terror,* p. 18.

31. The Septuagint adds the words "with her son Isaac."

32. Von Rad, *Genesis,* p. 227. Speiser agrees, insisting that "There is nothing in the text to suggest that he was abusing him, a motive deduced by many troubled readers in their effort to account for Sarah's anger" (*Genesis,* p. 155).

33. This is a reference to the accusation lodged against young Joseph by Potiphar's wife after she failed to seduce him.

34. Exod. 32:1–14 describes Israel's worship of the molten calf at Sinai.

35. In this scene the soldiers of Ishbosheth (the son of Israel's deceased king, Saul) and David's fighting men engage in a tournament ultimately leading to bloodshed.

36. Here, R. Simeon b. Yochai offers his own interpretation.

37. Genesis (Vayera) LIII 12, p. 470.

38. Brueggemann, *Genesis,* p. 183. See also Tamez, "The Woman Who Complicated," p. 9.

39. Wiesel, "Ishmael and Hagar," p. 246.

40. Genesis (Vayera) LIII 13, p. 472.

41. Modern commentators point out the similarities between the two Hagar episodes. In both Genesis 16 and Gen. 21:8–21, Sarah's outrage forces Hagar into the desert, where she converses with God's messenger. Many scholars believe that the two passages are variations of a single tradition, the former primarily from the Yahwistic source (except for vs. 1a, 3, and 15–16, which are attributed to the later Priestly editors), the latter the product of the Elohist. When both versions of the story were included as *separate* events, however, the conclusion of the Yahwistic version was changed so that Hagar did not remain in the desert, but rather returned to Abram's household for the birth of Ishmael. On differences between literary styles in Genesis 16 and 21, see McEvenue, "A Comparison of Narrative Styles," pp. 64–80.

42. Trible, *Texts of Terror,* p. 23. For Rashi, the verb's import was not confined to Hagar's physical movement. He believed that Hagar "strayed," that is, she returned to the idolatry of her youth (Rashi, *Commentaries on the Pentateuch,* p. 48).

43. In "Ishmael and Hagar," Wiesel notes: "Hagar always

refers to Ishmael as a *yeled*, a child; for the angel, and the text, Ishmael is a *na'ar*, a boy. Though he is seventeen years old, he is, in his mother's eyes, a child—a sick and unhappy child" (p. 245).

44. Trible, *Texts of Terror*, p. 25.

45. Von Rad, *Genesis*, p. 226.

46. Ginzberg, *Legends*, p. 265.

47. Trible, *Texts of Terror*, p. 17. Again, we recall Esther Fuch's point that, in biblical narrative, mothers are depicted as concerned first and foremost with the welfare of their sons.

48. Tamez, "The Woman Who Complicated," p. 16.

49. The words "she went and filled the skin with water" gave the rabbis an opportunity to criticize Hagar for lack of faith. They claimed that she filled the skin out of fear that the well would disappear (Genesis [Vayera] LIII 14, p. 474).

50. Note that in v. 16 Hagar sat a "bowshot" away from her son.

51. In *Midrash Rabbah* (Genesis [Vayera] LXIII 15, p. 474), we read "R. Isaac said: Throw a stick into the air, and it will fall back to its place of origin [the ground]. Thus, because it is written, *And she had a handmaid, an Egyptian, whose name was Hagar* . . . therefore it is written, AND HIS MOTHER TOOK HIM A WIFE OUT OF EGYPT.

52. Genesis (Chayye Sarah) LXI 4, pp. 542–543. This opinion was shared by Rashi, *The Soncino Chumash*, p. 132.

53. So Rashi, *The Soncino Chumash*, p. 132.

54. Gordon, "Hagar: A Throw-Away Character?"

55. Trible, *Texts of Terror*, p. 14. According to Wiesel, "Rabbi Shimon bar Yohai, a very great sage, envies her and says so in public. When he is in Rome on behalf of his brethren in occupied Judea, he exclaims: 'Hagar, a servant of my ancestors, was three times privileged to see an angel bearing a blessing—and I am here on a humanitarian mission and have seen no angel at all! Is that fair?' " ("Ishmael and Hagar," p. 244). The rabbis disagreed about how many angels addressed Hagar. See, for example, Genesis (Lech Lecha) XLV 7, p. 385.

56. Tamez, "The Woman Who Complicated," p. 13. Hence the Hagar episodes, for Tamez, do far more than simply heighten suspense by delaying the fulfillment of God's promise that Abram will have an heir through Sarah.

57. "Ishmael and Hagar," p. 241.

58. Ibid., p. 242.

59. Ibid., p. 240.

60. Ibid., p. 245.

61. Ibid., p. 247.

62. Ibid. Presupposed here is the identification of Ishmael as the ancestor of Arabic Muslims.

63. Ibid.

64. Ibid.

65. Ibid., p. 248.

66. Ibid.

67. Ibid., pp. 248–249.

68. Tamez, "The Woman Who Complicated," p. 6. It does not necessarily follow, however, that persons who *identify* with Sarah approve of everything that she does.

69. In *Sarah the Priestess,* Teubal understands Sarah's expulsion of Hagar and Ishmael against the background of her devotion to her Mesopotamian, matriarchal culture and her struggle against the patriarchy of Canaan. She had hoped to be "built up" through the son of her handmaiden (*šipchâ*). Because of Hagar's inappropriate attitude (16:4), however, Sarah reduced her to a simple slave (*'āmā*) and rejected Ishmael as her offspring. Ishmael's interaction with Isaac in 21:9 was no mere child's play. Rather, Teubal conjectures that it was in some sense sexual, related to the fact that Ishmael was circumcised, but Isaac was not. (Teubal disregards the notice of Isaac's circumcision in 21:4, which is from the Priestly editors.) Sarah abhored circumcision, Teubal speculates, because it was a threat to her matriarchal values. She expelled Ishmael and his mother from the household because they were an alien, patriarchal influence on her son. Teubal's study, which relies heavily upon inference and reading between the lines, provides Sarah with both strong sociocultural motivation, and legal precedent, for her actions.

70. Weems, *Just a Sister Away,* pp. 1–19.

71. Ibid., p. 2.

72. Ibid., p. 3.

73. Ibid., p. 10.

74. Ibid., p. 15.

75. Trible, *Texts of Terror,* p. 28.

76. Ibid.

77. Trible, *Texts of Terror,* p. 9; Weems, *Just A Sister Away,* pp. 11–12.

78. On the reproach of barrenness in the world of ancient Israel, see Bird, "Images of Women in the Old Testament," pp. 62–63.

79. Fuchs, "A Jewish Feminist Reading of the Hagar Stories," p. 8.

80. Ibid., p. 1.

81. Ibid., p. 8.

82. Ibid., pp. 5–7.

83. Ibid., p. 8.

84. This, Fuchs argues, is the problem with Trible's interpretation: "By describing the supposed power imbalance between Sarai and Hagar, Trible reinscribes the patriarchal constructions of female rivalry. By driving a hermeneutic wedge between Sarai and Hagar, by emphasizing the national/ethnic and class division ascribed to the characters, Trible recapitulates the strategies by which the biblical text draws the female characters apart" (ibid., p. 17).

85. Wiesel, "Ishmael and Hagar," pp. 247–248.

86. *El* was a common Semitic designation for deity.

87. Wiesel, "Ishmael and Hagar," p. 244.

5

More than
Just a Pretty Face:
Critical, Rabbinical,
and Feminist Perspectives
on Esther

Read the following four passages by twentieth-century interpreters of the book of Esther, and you may find it difficult to believe that they are all describing the same character:

Esther, for the chance of winning wealth and power, takes her place in the herd of maidens who become concubines of the king. She wins her victories not by skill or by character, but by her beauty. She conceals her origin, is relentless toward a fallen enemy (7:8–10), secures not merely that the Jews escape from danger, but that they fall upon their enemies, slay their wives and children, and plunder their property (8:11; 9:2–

10). Not satisfied with this slaughter, she asks that Haman's ten sons be hanged, and that the Jews may be allowed another day for killing their enemies in Susa (9:13–15). The only redeeming traits in her character are her loyalty to her people and her bravery in attempting to save them (4:16).[1]

The poignancy of Esther's plight is almost certainly the most gripping part of the *Megillah* in purely personal terms.[2] A Jewish girl hoping against hope not to become first lady of the world finds herself spending twelve months in an alien harem dedicated to the sole purpose of preparing for the king's pleasure. Then she is chosen queen and lives at the center of oriental intrigue and passion while guarding the secret of her origin and secretly holding fast to her religion.[3]

Buried in Esther's character is . . . full compliance with patriarchy. In contrast to Vashti, who refused to be men's sexual object and her husband's toy, Esther is the stereotypical woman in a man's world. She wins favor by the physical beauty of her appearance, and then by her ability to satisfy sexually. She concentrates on pleasing those in power, that is, men. . . . [4]

[Esther's] conduct throughout the story has been a masterpiece of feminine skill. From beginning to end, she does not make a misstep. . . . She is a model for the successful conduct of life in the often uncertain world of the Diaspora.[5]

Who Was Esther?

Both Esther and the book that bears her name have always generated strong, diverse opinions and interpretations. Some early Christians, thinking the story too nationalistic and inimical to Gentiles, opposed Esther's inclusion in their Bibles. No New Testament author referred to it, they argued; and the book explained the origins of a Jewish festival, Purim ("lots"), that had no Christian counterpart.[6]

Christians were not the first, however, to raise questions about Esther's inclusion within scripture. Although the scroll has always enjoyed widespread popularity among Jews,[7] it nevertheless prompted debate in at least some Jewish quarters: Why was it lacking even a single reference to YHWH, the God of Israel? Where was mention of Torah, prayer, covenant, or dietary restrictions?[8] Of the biblical books, Esther alone is not represented among the scrolls and fragments found at Qumran. And while Josephus[9] and the rabbinical authors of *Baba Bathra*[10] regarded the book as canonical, the Talmud bears witness that Esther's status was debated into the third or fourth centuries C.E.[11]

Who was Esther, and why was her story so controversial? The following hymn, recited by Jews during Purim, includes a poetic summary of the tale:[12]

> When Mordecai saw that evil was abroad,
>   and Haman's edicts were proclaimed in Shushan,
> he put on sackcloth and arranged for mourning,
>   ordained a fast and sat in ashes.
> "Who will arise to atone for error
>   and win forgiveness for our ancestors' sins?"
> A flower blossomed from the palm tree,
>   Hadassah [Esther] arose to stir those asleep.
> Her servants hastened to give Haman wine
>   that he might drink the venom of serpents.
> He rose through his wealth and fell through his
>   wickedness;
>   upon the gallows he built he himself was
>   hanged.

All the world was struck with amazement
  when Haman's *pur* became our Purim.[13]

For a fuller answer to our questions, however, we must turn to the biblical book itself. There we meet Esther and Mordecai, two members of the Jewish Diaspora[14] whose bravery, devotion, and ingenuity made possible the deliverance of their people from destruction during the reign of Ahasuerus, the Persian king who ruled from 485–464 B.C.E.[15]

Queen Vashti Is Deposed

Our story begins with an opulent show of self-indulgence. The scene is Susa, capital of the mighty Persian empire stretching "from India to Nubia."[16] After entertaining his nobles and governors during a one-hundred-and-eighty-day wine feast, King Ahasuerus hosts a second celebration for all the city's other inhabitants. Guests are entertained in rooms with fine wall hangings. Silver and gold furniture sits on mosaic floors studded with precious stones. Wine flows in abundance. It is, in short, an astonishing display.[17] Meanwhile, in a nearby suite of rooms, Queen Vashti fetes the female guests.

All this revelry is interrupted, however, when Ahasuerus flies into a furious rage. Queen Vashti has refused to parade her beauty before his besotted guests! How, Ahasuerus asks his closest advisers, can the king save face (Esth. 1:15)? Pleased by their advice, he issues a royal edict banishing the recalcitrant queen from his presence and ordering that every man be master of his own home (1:22). What other course of action, after all, can he choose? Failure to act could threaten the peace and stability of the entire kingdom (1:16), for Vashti's impudence would undoubtedly incite other women to disobey their husbands as well.[18]

Rabbinical Reflections on Scene One

This opening scene, with its extraordinary excesses and spontaneous, emotive acts, was certain to catch the rabbis' attention. They questioned, for example, the source of Ahasuerus's great wealth. Why was such a wicked man so prosperous? Esther Rabbah attributes to a certain Rabbi Tanchuma the view that Nebuchadrezzar, the Babylonian king who destroyed Jerusalem (including the Solomonic temple) and exiled many of its inhabitants, was the source of Ahasuerus's lucre:

Nebuchadnezzar, may he be crushed and exterminated, amassed all the money in the world, and he was very niggardly with it. So when he felt his end approaching, he said to himself: Why should I leave all this money to Evil-Merodach?[19] So he ordered big ships of brass to be made, and filled them with money and dug trenches and hid them by the Euphrates and turned the waters of the Euphrates over them. On the day that Cyrus decreed that the Temple should be built,[20] God revealed them to him, as it says, *Thus saith the Lord to His anointed, to Cyrus, whose right hand I have holden, to subdue nations before him . . . that the gates may not be shut* (Isa. XLV, 1) and further on it says, *And I will give thee the treasures of darkness, and hidden riches of secret places* (*ib.* 3).[21]

So it was Nebuchadrezzar's ill-gotten booty that Ahasuerus inherited and squandered on his guests! So boundless was his extravagance that each golden goblet was used only once, and no two were alike.[22] Every guest drank wine that was older than himself.[23]

Queen Vashti also drew the rabbis' attention. They did not, however, respect her willingness to defy this foolish, intemperate man. Many contemporary feminists applaud Vashti's boldness, urging women to emulate her, rather than the compliant Esther. Many of the rabbis thought her a villainess, however; and they provided her with a poisonous pedigree. Vashti was, they claimed, the daughter of wicked King Belshazzar, Daniel's nemesis, and the granddaughter of Nebuchadrezzar.[24] A zealous hater of the Jews, she insisted that Ahasuerus put an end to their efforts to rebuild the temple in Jerusalem.[25] Every Sabbath, the rabbis claimed, Vashti forced the Jewish women in her kingdom to strip off their clothes and work. That explains why Vashti was called to appear before the king "on the seventh day" (Esth. 1:10) and why he commanded her to appear in public without clothing. Such, you see, was the rabbi's understanding of the phrase "wearing a royal diadem" (1:11). They believed that Vashti was to appear wearing *only* the royal crown, in order that her beauty might be fully observed and appreciated.[26] Vashti declined, of course, but not out of modesty. No, the rabbis insisted that she refused to appear because God already had stricken her with leprosy as punishment for her sins; and she did not want her disease discovered.[27] A further Midrash makes the surprising claim that Vashti's fate was more horrible than the banishment (or confinement?) mentioned in verse 19 suggests. According to this view, the queen paid for her defiance with her life: "He gave the order," the Midrash states, "and they brought in her head on a platter."[28]

In the Talmud, we learn that the edict precipitated by Vashti's defiance actually saved the Jews from extinction.[29] How can this be? Because, one commentator explained, when the people heard it, they could not understand why so self-evident a decree should be issued. Of course a man's word was law in his own home! They became suspicious—perhaps the king was issuing edicts while in a drunken stupor! When a second edict appeared ordering the extermination of the Jews, the people feared that Ahasuerus had again acted while intoxicated and would reverse his order in the morning; and so they did nothing. But had they not feared royal reprisal, the rabbis said, they would have begun the slaughter immediately, instead of waiting until the designated day.[30]

Esther: History or Fiction?

Obviously, the rabbis believed that the book of Esther was a factual account of actual events that happened to real people. Certainly there is much in the book to commend such a view. The anonymous biblical author presents his work as if it were a straightforward recounting of facts. He begins with an introduction that is characteristic of biblical histories (see Esth. 1:1–3) and ends by referring his readers to another literary source that verifies the events he has related (see 10:2). Moreover, our knowledge of the Persian empire confirms many of the story's details, suggesting that the author was familiar with the customs and conditions of that day. Ahasuerus did, for example, have a winter palace at Susa; and he was well known for his drinking parties, extravagant gifts, and bellicose temper.[31] Moreover, a text dating from approximately the same period as our story mentions a government administrator at Susa named Marduka, the identical name underlying the hebraized Mordecai. (Possibly, however, the author of Esther selected a common name for his fictional character.)[32]

Nevertheless, contemporary biblical scholars question the book's historicity. Although some of its details are accurate, others are not. Ahasuerus did not, as the author appears to believe, rule soon—if not immediately—after the Babylonian king, Nebuchadrezzar II (605/604–562 B.C.E.). His wife's name was Amestris, not Vashti; and there is no evidence that he expelled her in order to marry a beautiful young Jewess. In fact, at the time when he was supposedly searching for Vashti's replacement, Ahasuerus was actually waging an unsuccessful military campaign against Greece.

Specialists have noted similarities between the fall of Vashti and legendary stories of harem intrigues, such as those found in *A Thousand and One Nights*.[33] One scholar has argued that the book of Esther was compiled from three originally independent stories: the harem legend of Vashti; the story of Mordecai, an individual caught up in intrigue, rivalry, and persecution in Susa; and the story of Esther, a young Jewess who was able, through her relationship with the king, to save her people from peril.[34] If there is history in any of these stories, some scholars believe, it resides in the Mordecai narratives, not only because of the reference to Marduka in an extrabiblical text, but also because both the book itself, and extrabiblical Jewish sources, emphasize Mordecai over Esther.[35] There is no extrabiblical evidence, however, supporting the historical veracity of Esther's plot. It is probably best, therefore, "to bracket such historical issues and to regard the book as the polished product of a master storyteller who combined suspense, irony, and drama in order to ground a popular Jewish festival in events of universal significance."[36]

Esther Becomes Queen

Some time later, the king's anger subsides and he "remembers" Vashti—with regret, perhaps.[37] Of course, her reinstatement (if, contrary to the rabbis' belief, she was still alive) is forbidden by the unchangeable law of Persia and Media (Esth. 1:19).[38] The king is pleased, however, by his servants' advice that the most beautiful maidens in his empire be taken into the royal harem so that the one most pleasing to him may reign in Vashti's place.[39] Among those brought to Susa is Esther (also called Hadassah, "myrtle"), a beautiful orphan raised by her older cousin, Mordecai, "son of Jair son of Shimei son of Kish, a Benjaminite" (2:5). Mordecai's patrilineage is not an inconsequential detail in the story for, as we shall see, it figures prominently in the unfolding plot.

According to the biblical text, Mordecai had been "carried away from Jerusalem among the captives carried away with Jeconiah king of Judah, whom Nebuchadnezzar king of Babylon had carried away" in 597 B.C.E. (2:6, RSV). Scholars are quick to point out that if this were actually the case, then Mordecai would be a very old Judean indeed. Even if he were only one day old when he was deported, he would still be approximately one hundred and fifteen years old when our story begins.[40] However, the biblical author either did not recognize, or was unconcerned by, this chronological difficulty.

Advised by her cousin not to reveal "her people or her kindred" (2:10), Esther wins the favor of Hegai, the eunuch in charge of the king's harem. After twelve months of beautifying treatments, each maiden spends a single night with the king.[41] When Esther's turn comes, Ahasuerus "loves" her more than all the others, and she is crowned queen.

The rabbis were horrified that Esther, a devout Jewess, was forced to marry a heathen king. One Targum detailed Mordecai's efforts to save her from so terrible a fate:

> Mordecai heard that virgins were being sought, and he removed Esther and hid her from the officers of King Xerxes, who had gone out to seek virgins, in order that they might not lead her away. And he hid her away in the closet of a bedroom, that the messengers of the king might not see her. But the daughters of the heathen, when the commissioners were sent, danced and showed their beauty at the windows; so that, when the King's messengers returned, they brought many virgins from the provinces. Now the King's messengers knew Esther; and when they saw that she was not among these virgins, they said one to another, We weary ourselves unnecessarily in the provinces, when there is in our own province a maiden fairer of face and finer of form that all the virgins that we have brought. So, when Esther was sought and was not

found, they made it known to King Xerxes, and he
wrote in dispatches, that every virgin who hid herself
from the royal messengers should be sentenced to
death. When Mordecai heard this, he was afraid, and
brought out Esther, the daughter of his father's
brother, to the market-place.[42]

Some of the rabbis, however, discerned in Mordecai's
reluctance more than simply the desire to keep Esther
out of a pagan king's harem. They believed that Mordecai
had taken his cousin to be his wife. The basis for this
startling opinion was found in 2:7, where we read that
"Mordecai adopted her as his own daughter." For *lĕbat,*
"as a daughter," these rabbis read *lĕbayith,* "for a house;"
and the word *bayith,* "house," can refer to one's wife in
rabbinic literature.[43]

Assassins at Court

Twice in three verses, we are told that Mordecai "sits at
the king's gate" (2:19–21, RSV). The expression is not an
indication of unemployment or laziness on Mordecai's
part. Rather, it was likely a technical phrase indicating his
status as a minor official in the royal court (note that
Ahasuerus uses the same phrase in 6:10). His proximity
to the harem allows Mordecai to keep informed of Esther's welfare; but it also enables him to learn of an assassination plot against the king devised by two disgruntled
officers, Bigthan and Teresh. Mordecai alerts Esther to
the danger; she, in turn, warns Ahasuerus in Mordecai's
name. The guilty servants are hanged,[44] and an account
of the events is "recorded in the Book of the Chronicles
in the presence of the king" (2:23, RSV).[45]
With the end of this scene, readers may well ponder
how events, whether fortuitously or providentially, have
conspired to bring us to this point: A banquet becomes

the occasion for a drunken king's dethronement of his queen. The search for a new queen places Esther within the palace and positions her cousin, Mordecai, to perform a significant, but as yet unrewarded, service for the king. Indeed, we leave this scene with a strong suspicion that the stage has been set, and the real plot of the play is about to begin.

Mordecai Outrages a Dangerous Foe

Enter Haman the Agagite who, having found favor with the king, is promoted to the exalted position of grand vizier. Henceforth, lesser officials must bow whenever he comes into sight. Mordecai, however, does not bow. What is the reason for this serious lapse of protocol?

Some rabbis believed that Mordecai declined on religious grounds, refusing to prostrate himself save before the God of Israel.[46] A glance at Genesis 42:6 suggests, however, that Jews bowed to kings and others of high rank. The explanation for Mordecai's obstinacy should rather be sought in the tradition of an ancient feud.[47] Mordecai's Benjaminite ancestry was, you will remember, carefully established in Esther 2:5. His tribal roots linked Mordecai to a venerable forebear—Saul, Israel's first king.[48] According to 1 Samuel 15, YHWH commanded Saul, through the prophet Samuel, to march against King Agag and the Amalekites and utterly to eradicate them, slaying "men and women, infants and sucklings, oxen and sheep, camels and asses" (15:3). Since the days of Moses and Joshua, Israel had suffered at the hands of the Amalekites.[49] Now, Saul was in a position to rid his nation of an age-old, dangerous enemy. The battle was fought, and Israel's army emerged victorious. But King Saul decided against the annihilation God had ordered:

[7]Saul destroyed Amalek from Havilah all the way to

Shur, which is close to Egypt, [8]and he captured King Agag of Amalek alive. He proscribed all the people, putting them to the sword; [9]but Saul and the troops spared Agag and the best of the sheep, the oxen, the second-born, the lambs, and all else that was of value. They would not proscribe them; they proscribed only what was cheap and worthless (1 Sam. 15:7–9).

When Samuel learned what Saul had done, he denounced him and killed King Agag himself (15:33). But before he could do so, the rabbis taught, Agag spent one last night with his wife. She conceived and gave birth. And generations later, a descendant of Agag's youngest child was born. His name as Haman. So, you see, Mordecai the Benjaminite refused to bow before Haman the Agagite, because Haman's ancestor had led to Saul's undoing.[50]

Haman's Deadly Plan

Enraged by his enemy's defiance, Haman "disdain[s] to lay hands on Mordecai alone" (Esth. 3:6). Instead, he devises a pogrom against all Jews throughout the empire.[51] In the first month, Nisan, a *pur* ("lot") is cast in Haman's presence to determine a propitious month and day for his vicious scheme.[52] At last, it falls favorably on the twelfth month, Adar.[53] Haman then exercises his powers of persuasion on the king, convincing him to eliminate "a certain people" who adhere to their own laws but abrogate the laws of the empire. To sweeten the pot a bit, Haman offers to pay ten thousand talents of silver to the king's treasury, lest the loss of Jewish taxes diminish the king's revenues. Ahasuerus, true to his unreflective self, simply gives his grand vizier permission to do with the Jews "as you see fit" (3:11).[54] Their agreement is sealed when the king removes his signet ring and hands it to Haman, this "son of Hammedatha the Agagite, the foe of the Jews" (3:10). Although the thirteenth of Adar is almost a year away, an edict is published immediately, granting non-Jews permission on that day "to destroy, massacre, and exterminate all the Jews, young and old, children and women, . . . and to plunder their possessions" (3:13). The scene concludes with a grim contrast: The citizens of Susa are dumbfounded by this decree, but Ahasuerus and Haman sit down to drink (3:15).

Why was Haman's decree proclaimed so far in advance of the appointed day? The rabbis identified several reasons for his haste. Some said that Haman feared his fickle king would have a change of heart. Once his petition was granted, he wanted it to become law immediately. Others suggested that Haman simply wished to prolong the Jews' agony by informing them of their impending massacre well in advance. Also expressed, however, was the view that God desired a lapse of so many months in order to allow the children of Israel a chance to repent.[55] Of what sin, you ask? Of the sin incurred when the Jews not only attended Ahasuerus's banquet (presumably they were forced to go), but also enjoyed it.[56]

"Who Knows Whether You Have Not Come to the Kingdom for Such a Time as This?"

When Mordecai discovers Haman's scheme, he appears in public wearing sackcloth and ashes (signs of mourning and/or humiliation) and crying aloud in the streets. His actions, the narrator informs us, are mirrored in the reactions of Jews throughout the provinces as they, too, learn of the murderous edict (Esth. 4:3).

Having passed thus through the city streets, Mordecai must stop at the palace door, because persons wearing sackcloth are forbidden entrance.[57] When Esther learns of his appearance and behavior, she is "greatly distressed" and sends him clothes, but Mordecai refuses them.[58] As a result, their conversation must transpire through a messenger. Mordecai urges his cousin to approach the king and entreat him on behalf of her people, but Esther responds by giving him a deadly serious lesson in palace protocol:

> [11]"All the king's courtiers and the people of the king's provinces know that if any person, man or woman, enters the king's presence in the inner court without having been summoned, there is but one law for him— that he be put to death. Only if the king extends the golden scepter to him may he live. Now I have not been summoned to visit the king for the last thirty days" (Esth. 4:10).

Not summoned by the king for thirty days! Have their years of marriage cooled his ardor? Has there been a quarrel, some rupture in the royal marriage that makes an initiative by Esther at this time especially dangerous?

Mordecai's response to Esther is a masterful piece of rhetoric, for he combines self-interest with a challenge to participate in a noble—indeed, providential—cause. " 'Think not that in the king's palace you will escape any more than all the other Jews,' " he warns. " 'For if you keep silence at such a time as this, relief and deliverance will rise for the Jews from another quarter, but you and your father's house will perish. And who knows whether you have not come to the kingdom for such a time as this?' " (4:13–14, RSV). Esther meets this challenge, promising to go before the king. In preparation for so hazardous a deed, however, she orders Mordecai to ensure that all the Jews in Susa join her in a three-day fast.

According to one Midrash, when Mordecai received Esther's instructions to fast he protested, saying, "But these three days of fasting include the first day of Passover" (when fasting is not permitted). But she replied, "If

there is no Israel, why should there be a Passover?"[59]
Obviously Esther, like her cousin, could wield some powerful rhetoric; and Mordecai was forced to agree.

The rabbis did not criticize Esther for her initial reluctance to jeopardize her life. On the contrary, they praised
her for her perceptiveness. Esther was hesitant to appear
unbidden before the king, they explained, because doing
so would force Ahasuerus to decide either to have her
killed on the spot or to allow her to live. If he did the
latter, she would already owe her life to the king's for-
bearance. How, then, could she ask for even more clem-
ency, this time on behalf of her people? Rather, Esther
reasoned that the king, who had not visited her for a
month, would certainly come to her chambers soon. At
that time, she would be in a more advantageous position
to make her petition.[60]

Esther Before the King

Beautiful in her royal robes, Esther approaches the in-
ner court of Ahasuerus's palace. When her husband spies
her, he extends the golden scepter immediately, inquires
concerning her welfare, and hyperbolically promises to
grant her any wish, "even to half the kingdom" (Esth.
5:3). But rather than entreat on behalf of her people,
Esther invites both Ahasuerus and Haman to a banquet.
Quickly, the grand vizier is located; and as they enjoy
their wine feast, the king again asks Esther's petition.
Once more she demurs, however, imploring only that
both men return for yet another feast on the following
day, when her request will be revealed.

Why does Esther delay? Will her opportunity to inter-
vene on her people's behalf be lost if she continues to
evade the king's questions? Modern scholars suggest that
Esther's suspension of her request is, in fact, a way of
creating suspense for the reader. Moreover, the narrator

needs time to put key pieces of the story (e.g., Mordecai's exaltation) in place before the plot's denouement. For their part, however, the rabbis believed that Esther was very wise to chose so circuitous a route toward her goal. When Haman arrived at her first banquet, they explained, he was suspicious of the queen's attention: Was there some connection between this invitation and his recent edict concerning the Jews? Leaving the party, however, Haman was thrilled by the flattery and fellowship he had enjoyed. Disarmed, he was unprepared for the outcome of Esther's second banquet.[61]

On his way home, Haman's ebullient mood is dampened by the sight of Mordecai—standing erect, obstinate as ever. His good humor returns, however, when his wife, Zeresh, and friends suggest that he construct a fifty-cubit tall gallows and obtain the king's permission to hang Mordecai upon it before tomorrow's feast (see 5:14).

According to one rabbinical commentator, Haman's wife and friends suggested a towering gallows in order that he might enjoy the sight of Mordecai hanging from it while he feasted with the king and queen.[62] He searched for, but could not find, so lengthy a piece of wood within Susa. So he sent for his son Parshandasa, governor of the Mt. Ararat region, who procured for his father a beam from the remains of Noah's ark (identified in Gen. 6:15 as fifty cubits wide).[63]

Mordecai's Reward

Unable to sleep, King Ahasuerus orders that excerpts from the Royal Annals be read to him. When he realizes that Mordecai has not yet been rewarded for exposing the conspiracy against his life, Ahasuerus asks Haman (at court, though it be the middle of the night), "What should be done for a man whom the king desires to honor?" Haman temporarily tables his request to hang

Mordecai, for he espies in the monarch's question an opportunity to heap further glory upon himself. After all, he reasons, "Whom would the king desire to honor more than me?" (6:6). He therefore specifies the reward that he would most relish: that he be clothed in royal robes, set astride a horse that wears a royal crown,[64] and paraded through the city square. The sweet taste of anticipated glory turns to bile, however, when Haman learns that Mordecai, his bitter enemy, is "the man whom the king desires to honor," while *he*, Haman, must lead him through the streets of Susa.

In the Talmud, we read that as Haman was escorting Mordecai around the city square, Haman's daughter spied them from an overhanging roof. Thinking that the man on the horse was her father, and the servant leading him was Mordecai, she took her chamber pot and dumped it on her father's head. He looked up, revealing her mistake, and Haman's daughter threw herself off the roof and died.[65]

His ordeal over at last, a humiliated Haman covers his head and returns home. He tells Zeresh and his friends all that has befallen him; and they, sounding "for all the world as if they were a Greek tragic chorus,"[66] foretell his demise: " 'If Mordecai, before whom you have begun to fall, is of Jewish stock, you will not overcome him; you will fall before him to your ruin' " (6:13b).

Why did his wife and advisers (no longer called "his friends," the rabbis noted, since they cared for him only so long as he had power) speak such discouraging words to an already crestfallen Haman? Because, the early commentators explained, they knew that Mordecai's rise was not coincidental, and Haman's downfall was sure to follow.[67] According to the Talmud, "R. Judah b. Illa'i drew a lesson from this verse, saying: Why are two fallings mentioned here?[68] Haman's friends said to him: This people is likened to the dust and it is likened to the stars. When they go down, they go down to the dust, and when they rise they rise to the stars."[69]

The Villain Becomes a Victim

When the king and Haman gather for a second banquet, Esther finally reveals her petition, imploring that her life and the lives of her people be spared.[70] Ahasuerus is enraged to discover that his grand vizier has doomed the Jews to destruction, massacre, and extermination (see Esth. 7:4); and Haman trembles with fright before the royal couple. The rabbis explained why he was so afraid:

> In the presence of both of them, together, he trembled. Had he been confronted by either of them privately, he could have talked his way out of the bind. To the Queen he could have innocently pleaded that he did not know the Jews were her people, and had he known he would never have issued the decree. To the King he could have claimed that, although the Jews were Esther's people, they were nevertheless worthy of extinction. But since both the King and Queen were there he couldn't defend himself: How could he tell the King—in the Queen's presence—that her people were evil? And how could he say to the Queen—in the King's presence—that, had he known they were her people, he never would have condemned them? Having said they were thoroughly evil it would have been traitorous for him to allow their survival![71]

While Ahasuerus is out in the palace garden (struggling to control his temper?), Haman prostrates himself upon Queen Esther's couch and begs for his life. The king reenters the room, however, and seeing Haman on top of the queen, concludes that he is trying to rape her: " 'Does he mean,' cried the king, 'to ravish the queen in my own palace?' " (7:8). Ahasuerus's anger signals his vizier's fate, and Haman's face is covered (probably standard treatment for condemned persons).[72] Harbonah, a servant of the king, alerts his master both to the gallows Haman has erected and to its intended victim; and Ahasuerus orders that the Agagite himself be hung upon it.[73] This reversal of expectation, such that "the villain suffers the fate of his intended victim," will recur in the following scene.[74]

Haman's Unalterable Edict

That very day, King Ahasuerus confers Haman's entire estate upon Esther. To Mordecai he entrusts his own signet ring, naming him grand vizier in Haman's place. When Esther appoints Mordecai to take charge of their former rival's possessions, he gains material wealth equal to his newfound political power. A problem remains, however, for the danger posed by Haman's unchangeable decree outlives him. Esther therefore must beseech the king on her people's behalf a second time:

> [5]"If it please Your Majesty," she said, "and if I have won your favor and the proposal seems right to Your Majesty, and if I am pleasing to you[75]—let dispatches be written countermanding those which were written by Haman son of Hammedatha the Agagite, embodying his plot to annihilate the Jews throughout the king's provinces. [6]For how can I bear to see the disaster which will befall my people! And how can I bear to see the destruction of my kindred!" (Esth. 8:5–6).

Ahasuerus grants Esther and Mordecai permission to write, "as [they] see fit" (8:8), a second edict regarding the Jews. This decree is quickly distributed by the king's swiftest horses throughout the one hundred and twenty-seven provinces of the empire, in languages appropriate to each region. The second degree does not abrogate the first, for how could it change the unchangeable law? It does, however, supplement it, granting the Jews permission not only to defend themselves, but also to strike back at anyone who threatens them:[76] "If any people or province attacks them, they may destroy, massacre, and exterminate its armed force together with women and children, and plunder their possessions" (8:11b). In these admittedly savage words, we recognize yet another reversal of the destinies of intended victims and perpetrators. These are, you see, the same words used to describe what Haman ordered done to the Jews in his initial edict (3:13).

When Mordecai emerges from the king's presence that day, his appearance has changed considerably. Now he is clothed in "royal robes of blue and white, with a magnificent crown of gold and a mantle of fine linen and purple wool" (8:15). Was it wrong for Mordecai to accept such magnificent clothing? Should he have despised the opulence of this pagan court, as did Esther?[77] No, the rabbis replied. Mordecai merited fine apparel, for in a time of crisis he willingly wore sackcloth and ashes. Because he rent his garments for his people's sake, he deserved garments fit for royalty. Having put dust upon his head, he was deserving of a gold crown.[78]

The city of Susa rejoices over this turn of events, and "the Jews [enjoy] light and gladness, happiness and honor" (8:16).[79] Feasting and celebration commence among Jews throughout the provinces; and some Gentiles also claim to be Jewish, since "the fear of the Jews had fallen upon them" (8:17).[80]

In the midst of great celebration, then, this scene comes to an end. Many modern scholars argue that, at an earlier stage in its history, the whole book of Esther actually ended at 8:17.[81] After all, the major component in its plot—the conflict between Haman and Mordecai—has been resolved by that point; and the threat to the Jews has ostensibly ended as well. Who would fight against them, given the power wielded by Esther and Mordecai and the right of Jews to harm anyone opposing them?

Nevertheless, in its canonical form, the book goes on to detail Jewish victories over their enemies and to sanction the celebration of Purim as an ongoing Jewish obligation.

The Jews Are Victorious

When the thirteenth of Adar arrives, fighting erupts both in Susa and throughout the provinces, and—again, the author relishes a reversal—on the day when "the enemies of the Jews had expected to get them in their power, the opposite happened, and the Jews got their enemies in their power" (9:1). The sudden appearance of multiple, hostile foes is surprising. How has a lone opponent, Haman, suddenly been replaced by a host of adversaries? Modern commentators who support the essential historicity of Esther's story explain that the growth of anti-Semitism in the months after Haman's edict was issued simply reflects the lamentable human disposition toward enmity motivated by avarice and fear of the "other."[82] It is possible, however, that the original story, ending at 8:17, was expanded by a subsequent author, who intensified opposition to the Jews in order to explain the origins and significance of the Jewish festival called Purim.[83]

Throughout the provinces, seventy-five thousand adversaries are slain. Even in Susa, where news of Mordecai's promotion had been received with great joy, the Jews kill five hundred men, including Haman's ten sons (9:6). Three times we are told that the Jews did not exercise their legal right (see 8:11) to seize their opponents' possessions. Most modern commentators follow the rabbis in perceiving here a setting right of King Saul's misguided decision to claim the best of the Amalekites' belongings.[84] Mordecai and his generation do not repeat the mistakes of the past.

Although the Jews of the provinces desist from warfare after a single day, Queen Esther obtains Ahasuerus's permission for the Jews in Susa to continue fighting on the fourteenth of Adar as well. Three hundred additional men die at their hands. Moreover, Ahasuerus grants Esther's request that Haman's dead sons be publicly hung (or impaled). This, Esther's final recorded petition to her husband, has earned her a strong rebuke from some modern commentators (see, for example, the first quotation at the beginning of this chapter). The rabbinical commentators defended her, however, claiming that Esther wished " . . . to frighten the enemies of Jewry throughout the realm . . . and to destroy Haman's staunchest supporters. She claimed that this was the only guarantee that the surviving enemies would not attempt to avenge their comrades on the following day."[85]

According to the book of Esther, this "historical" situation explains why Purim is a two-day celebration. Although the Jews living in the provinces celebrated their victory on the fourteenth of Adar, the Jews of Susa could not celebrate until the fifteenth. Lewis Bayles Paton was undoubtedly correct, however, when he observed in his commentary that here "history arises from custom, not custom from history."[86]

The Festival of Purim

In compliance with regular court procedure, these momentous events are officially recorded by Mordecai, who enjoins upon Jews the annual, ongoing observance of both the fourteenth and fifteenth days of Adar. Their celebrations shall consist of "feasting and merrymaking," as well as "sending gifts to one another and presents to the poor" (Esth. 9:22b). To these obligations the Jews commit themselves wholeheartedly. "Consequently," we read, "these days are recalled and observed in every generation: by every family, every province, and every city. And these days of Purim shall never cease among the

Jews, and the memory of them shall never perish among their descendants" (9:28). The emphasis upon Mordecai's written instructions, along with the legal style of verses 26–28, betrays the author's intent to convince his readers that Purim observance is obligatory among Jews, even though it has no basis in the Torah.[87] A second letter, written by Queen Esther, bestows her full authority upon Purim observance as well.

Our story ends with a reminder that the mighty deeds of King Ahasuerus are recorded in the "Annals of the Kings of Media and Persia" (10:2). Alongside this powerful man stands Mordecai, whose influence, exercised on behalf of his kindred, ensures their welfare. No reference is made, however, to Queen Esther.

Esther Among the Early Jews, and Additions to Her Story

We began this chapter with the question "Who was Esther?" In the course of telling her story, we have discovered how the rabbis answered it. Esther was the ideal Jewish woman: Modest, beautiful, and obedient, she remained faithful both to her God and to her people in the face of life-threatening danger. Torn from her beloved cousin (and husband?), she endured marriage to a pagan king and the excesses of his palace. When her people were faced with destruction, Esther's response was swift and intelligent—downright clever.

In their interpretations, of course, the rabbis frequently went beyond what was literally stated in the text. Unless readers know, for example, the rabbinical tendency to speak of one's wife as "my house," the suggestion that Mordecai married his cousin is unlikely ever to suggest itself. Moreover, there is no explicit support for the rabbinical view that Esther refused to transgress Jewish dietary standards or to work on the Sabbath. Neither does the text claim that she detested her royal robes, wearing them only to increase her chances for a favorable reception by the king. Yet because the commentators prized Esther so highly (and because they assumed that Jewish customs in her time were no different from orthodox Jewish practices, both religious and ethical, in their own day), the rabbis presupposed that Esther behaved precisely as they believed exemplary Jewish women should.

The rabbis also recognized that the book of Esther does not explicitly mention YHWH, the God of Israel. They nevertheless found allusions to God encoded in the text. They insisted, for example, that while references to "King Ahasuerus" had only the earthly monarch in view, references to "the king" alluded to YHWH, the heavenly King, as well as to Ahasuerus.[88] Moreover, they noted that the first Hebrew letters of the four Hebrew words translated "Let Your Majesty and Haman come today" (Esth. 5:4) form YHWH, the four consonants in the divine name (*Yahweh*). Obviously, the rabbis were aware of the absence of overt religious elements within the scroll but still were able to read and understand it as an explicitly religious story.[89]

At some early stage in the book's history, however, unknown Jewish readers of Esther decided to add those religious elements lacking in the Hebrew text. When we turn to Esther in the Septuagint,[90] we discover a number of additions distributed at points throughout the story. These "Additions to Esther," consisting of one hundred and seven verses, serve several functions.[91] Notably, however, they make explicit the religious elements that the rabbis could only presuppose, or find encoded, in their Hebrew text. In Addition A, for example, we learn of Mordecai's dream about two great dragons who roar against each other and about a righteous nation, prepared to die and crying out to God. In Addition F, the last in the book, Mordecai interprets this dream, realizing that the two dragons were Haman and himself and that YHWH has rescued the Jews. Addition C contains the prayers of Esther and Mordecai prior to her initial unbidden appearance before the king; Addition D explains how God intervened to transform Ahasuerus's initial anger at seeing her into tenderness. You can plainly see, therefore, that Greek-speaking readers who knew Esther as the book appears in the Septuagint, rather than in Hebrew Bibles, noticed no lack of religious concerns and references to the deity.

Feminist Interpretations of Esther

Not long ago, a Jewish friend bemoaned her daughter's delight in dressing up as Esther for the children's annual Purim celebration. "I tell her, 'Don't be Esther; be Vashti!' " she said. "I want her to be strong and independent, not passive and compliant."

Many contemporary feminists share my friend's opinion of Esther. Some modern scholars have even expressed surprise that the book bears her name, since they believe that Mordecai is the main character, the author's major concern. They wonder if Esther is anything more than just a pretty face. Vashti, however, is a completely different story.[92] Quite the beauty herself, her compliance with patriarchy had a limit. Disobedience led to banishment, of course, but more than just disobedience was at issue. As Alice Laffey writes,

> Vashti's banishment is not because of her disobedience but because of the potential effects of her disobedience. If Vashti were not punished, her decision could be the start of a major revolution. Other women might

look to her as their model; her example would then empower them to rebel against the domination of their husbands. She was cast off because she was an enormous threat to the patriarchal status quo.[93]

Laffey further suggests that Esther's story may have been told during a period when upper-class Israelite women were beginning to chafe at traditional societal roles and restrictions. If that is true, then the beginning of Esther sent an unequivocal message: Do not challenge the system, or you also will be cut off.[94]

Marjory Zoet Bankson likewise believes that Vashti's story was told to obviate the threat posed by uppity women. "What happened to Vashti was meant to be a lesson other women would not forget," Bankson writes. "They knew that Vashti had rejected the unspoken trade of sexuality for physical security. Vashti's elimination was meant to warn other women against doing what she had done. But her action implied that there was something more important in her life than existence alone."[95] Bankson's praise is not unqualified. She suggests, for example, that Vashti's decision to refuse Ahasuerus may have been made a bit hastily. But she nonetheless joins with those who wish to claim and emulate her:

> Vashti's story, meant to be a warning against saying such a "No!," has just the opposite effect from what was intended. It gives me an invitation to say "No!" when my body is about to be violated. I feel proud of Vashti's refusal. I love her reckless strength. I know the cost of such replies, where brute strength and economic power threaten life itself sometimes, but something in her act meets [a] longing in myself.[96]

Is Vashti the only appropriate role model for contemporary women in the book? Should we indeed urge our daughters to "be Vashti" rather than Esther? Or is Esther's way of dealing with the crises she faces also an honorable alternative for moderns? As we have seen, Laffey's answer to these questions is no. Not only did Esther rely upon her looks and sexuality to get ahead, but also she failed to plead the cause of her predecessor: "Rather than defend Vashti's decision and protest the injustice of her banishment," Laffey writes, "Esther uses Vashti's rejection for her own benefit. When feminists compare the two women, they extol Vashti, though they are not at all surprised that the literature, produced as it was in a patriarchal culture, honors Esther and relegates Vashti to oblivion. Their concern, however, is to reclaim Vashti."[97] One can, I suspect, ask whether Esther reasonably should be charged with "us[ing] Vashti's rejection for her own benefit." After all, the text clearly states that she "was taken" into the king's palace; one can presume that she had little choice in the matter and little opportunity to lecture the king on any subject. It is by no means clear, therefore, that the burden of defending Vashti before her husband can fairly be shifted onto Esther's shoulders. So while claiming Vashti as a role model is an exceedingly important undertaking, the question remains whether she *alone* deserves our respect.

In a recent article, Sidnie Ann White defends Esther against charges of selfish compliance, or cowardice, or both.[98] She argues for a contextual reading of Esther— one that takes seriously both the precarious position of Jews living in the Diaspora and the additional vulnerability of Esther, a woman living among the most powerful (and intemperate) men in Persia. Once we recognize the danger of Esther's situation, White claims, her actions can be understood as the intelligent, measured deeds of a woman seeking safety for both her people and herself.[99] Mordecai's actions, on the other hand, are ill-conceived and inappropriate to his circumstances; and they lead to near-ruinous results:

One can make the assumption that Mordecai had a good reason for refusing to bow down [before Ha-

man], but this remains an assumption. On the face of
it, however, Mordecai's refusal appears foolish. He
seems to have nothing to gain by it and a great deal to
lose. Surely this is not the action of a wise courtier! . . .
Then, having precipitated this crisis, he must rely on
Esther to undo the damage.[100]

When Esther reminds Mordecai that an uninvited appearance before the king can be fatal, she is not being
cowardly. She is simply stating a fact.[101] Reminded of her
obligation to her relatives and to the Jewish people as a
whole, however, she acts immediately, despite grave personal risk.[102] So exemplary is her behavior in the face of
every challenge that Esther is, in fact, a model for diaspora Jews: "By accepting the reality of a subordinate position and learning to gain power by working within the
structure rather than against it," White concludes, "the
Jew can build a successful and fulfilling life in the Diaspora, as Esther does in the court of Ahasuerus."[103]

Conclusion

We began this chapter by reading four quite different perspectives on Queen Esther. In the course of
telling her story, these various viewpoints have been
fleshed out, and we have recognized how each might be
defended—even if, in the end, we decide to reject one or
more as inappropriate. In addition, we have encountered
quite different appraisals of Vashti and Mordecai. Only
Haman commands unanimous disdain.

What perspectives will emerge from your mental and
spiritual wrestlings with Esther and her story? Will you
choose to reject her in favor of her predecessor, or will
you embrace her, dismissing Vashti as the imprudent wife

of an imprudent man? Possibly neither extreme is necessary or even wise. Contemporary readers may very well profit from the examples of both women. Vashti's courage in the face of unreasonable demands is certainly admirable. But Vashti undoubtedly attained the royal diadem because she, too, knew how to finesse life in a patriarchal culture. Had we visited her one day before her refusal to attend the king's party, we might have thought her a mere "product of her times," a "stereotypical woman in a man's world."[104] Esther, it is true, relied on more subtle strategies to affect the outcome of events. Sometimes, however, nonconfrontational approaches work best. Moreover, Esther also may have refused the king's wishes during some future disagreement. We simply do not know, since the author(s) of her story apparently did not write a sequel. This much, however, is certain: In the face of crises, oppression, and danger, different people—women and men—respond differently. Their actions are influenced by the times in which they live and by cultural conditioning, of course. But they also reflect their individual personalities, as well as their respective stages of growth, maturity, and self-awareness.

Literature—stories, poems, fables, and so on—can play a powerful role in shaping our responses to important experiences in our lives. Reading about a character's reaction to an extraordinary situation, we may wonder how we would respond to such an event. Faced with an important decision, we may, consciously or unconsciously, be influenced by the fates of literary characters who made choices under similar circumstances.

But if literature can influence us, providing a foretaste of life's experiences, broadening our horizons, and bringing us into contact with situations and ideas we might never otherwise encounter, then it must be recognized for the powerful tool that it is. Wise readers bring to all literature a hermeneutic of suspicion, recognizing that no literary work is unbiased, without an agenda, or utterly objective. Confronted by a host of literary role models, for example, women and men must decide for themselves to what extent, if any, those models are worthy of emulation.

The diverse perspectives of other readers who have wrestled with a character or story can assist in our own evaluative processes. Interpretive literature, too, broadens our thinking beyond the limits of our own inevitably limited ideas and judgments. As we have seen in this book, however, different interpreters of the same literary work can form astonishingly diverse opinions. If we limit the range of interpretive options that inform our own reflections—if, for example, we read only the ideas of "people like us"—we deprive ourselves of insight that could inform and enrich our own perspectives. For the sake of fresh ideas, sound critiques, and ongoing personal growth, then, literary interpretation—including biblical interpretation—must be a dialogue among members of more than a single constituency.

Notes

1. Paton, *The Book of Esther,* p. 96.
2. In Jewish tradition, the word *Megillah* ("scroll") usually refers to the book of Esther. The plural, *Megilloth* (or *Megillahs*), refers to the five scrolls—Song of Songs, Ruth, Lamentations, Ecclesiastes (also called Qoheleth), and Esther—associated with festivals during the Jewish liturgical year.
3. Scherman, "An Overview/The Period and the Miracle," in Zlotowitz, ed., *The Megillah/The Book of Esther,* p. xxxi.
4. Laffey, *An Introduction to the Old Testament,* p. 216.
5. White, "Esther: A Feminine Model for Jewish Diaspora," p. 173.
6. Among the early churches in the East (e.g., Anatolia and Syria), resistance to Esther was strong; in the West (e.g., Rome and Carthage), Esther was generally accepted as canonical. Although the early church eventually accepted Esther in its canon, resistence to it did not vanish altogether. Martin Luther, for example, declared, "I am so hostile to this book [II Maccabees] and to Esther that I could wish they did not exist at all; for they judaize too greatly and have much pagan impropriety" (*Table Talk,* xxiv). See Moore's helpful discussion of Esther's status among early Christians in *Esther,* p. XXV–XXXI.
7. In *Megillat Esther* (p. 15), Gordis notes that some medieval Jewish artists even relaxed the prohibition against depicting the human form in order to produce lavish illuminated manuscripts of the Esther scroll.
8. In "Wisdom in the Book of Esther" (pp. 419–455), Talmon argues that Esther is an historicized wisdom story which, like Ecclesiastes, Job, and parts of Proverbs (also wisdom literature), lacks references to specific Jewish religious practices.

9. A first-century (about 37–100 C.E.) Jewish historian, Flavius Josephus, is a major ancient source for Jewish history from 167 B.C.E. to 73 C.E. See *The Interpreter's Dictionary of the Bible*, s.v. "Josephus, Flavius"; also Moore, *Esther*, pp. XXII–XXIII.

10. This writing, now included in the Talmud, is generally dated to the second century C.E. The list appears in a *Baraitha* (a dictum not incorporated into the Mishnah) in *Baba Bathra 14b–15a*.

11. *Megillah 7a*, pp. 35–36; and *Sanhedrin*, p. 677. See also Moore, *Esther*, pp. XXIV–XXV.

12. Like the poem about the accomplished woman (Prov. 31:10–31), this hymn is an acrostic. See above, chapter one, n. 1.

13. Quoted in Gordis, *Megillat Esther*, p. 95.

14. The term "diaspora" is used to refer to Jews living outside the land of Israel.

15. Also called Xerxes I, Ahasuerus was the fourth king in the Achaemenian Period (550–331 B.C.E.) of Persian history.

16. Esth. 1:1.

17. In *Just a Sister Away* (p. 100), Weems observes that the biblical narrator, "in what might have been a subtle criticism of the king's self-indulgent tastes and hedonistic appetite, sneaks in a private tour of the palace."

18. Esth. 1:16–20.

19. Nebuchadrezzar's successor to the throne, Evil-merodach (562–560 B.C.E.) is cited in 2 Kings 25:27 (see also Jer. 52:31–34) for improving the living conditions of Judah's exiled king, Jehoiachin.

20. Cyrus of Persia defeated the Babylonians in a battle at Opis in 539 B.C.E. Shortly thereafter, the city of Babylon surrendered without resistence. Cyrus' edict permitting the exiled Judeans to return to Jerusalem and rebuild the Solomonic temple appears in Ezra 1:2–4 (in Hebrew; see also 2 Chron. 36:23) and Ezra 6:3–5 (in Aramaic).

21. Esther Rabbah II 3, pp. 33–34.

22. According to Esther Rabbah II 11, among Ahasuerus's goblets were the vessels removed from the temple in Jerusalem. So beautiful were they that when they were placed alongside other vessels, the latter "lost colour and became like lead" (p. 40).

23. *The Megillah/The Book of Esther*, p. 44.

24. *Seder Hadoros*, quoted in *The Megillah/The Book of Esther*, p. 45.

25. According to Esther Rabbah V 2, pp. 69–70, "she used to say to him, 'Do you seek to build what my ancestors destroyed?'" The identification of Ahasuerus with Artaxerxes (Ezra 4:1–24) is presupposed.

26. Esther Rabbah III 13, p. 54.

27. *The Megillah/The Book of Esther*, p. 46.

28. Esther Rabbah IV 11, p. 63.

29. *Megillah 12b*, pp. 72–73.

30. This opinion is cited in *The Megillah/The Book of Esther*, p. 52, and derives from *Me'am Loez*, an extremely popular eighteenth-century commentary written in Ladino (Judeo-Spanish). It was begun by Jacob Culi and carried on by others after his death.

31. Moore, *Esther*, p. XLI.

32. Ibid., p. L.

33. Ibid., *Esther*, p. L.

34. Bardtke, *Das Buch Esther*, pp. 249–252.

35. 2 Maccabees 14:36 refers to "the day of Mordecai," but says nothing at all about Esther. See Moore, *Esther*, pp. LI–LIII.

36. Darr, "Esther and Additions to Esther," p. 177.

37. See Moore, *Esther*, p. 17.

38. See also Dan. 6:16; Darius the Mede was unable to save Daniel from the lion's den because Daniel prayed to his God in violation of "the law of the Medes and Persians that may not be abrogated."

39. According to 2:3, Ahasuerus was advised to "appoint officers in every province of your realm to assemble all the beautiful young virgins." The rabbis explained that this procedure was followed because locals would know immediately who were the most comely women in their region and so could facilitate the selection process (*The Megillah/The Book of Esther*, p. 53).

40. *Tanakh*, following older commentators, solves the problem by understanding the relative pronoun ("who") at the beginning of v. 6 to refer to Kish. But see Moore, *Esther*, pp. 26–27.

41. The Bible tells us that during this time of preparation,

Esther was allotted "seven maids who were her due from the king's palace" (2:9). In the opinion of at least one commentator, these seven maids were inadvertently helpful to Esther in her attempts to keep her Jewish identity a secret: "Forever mindful that . . . *laziness leads to indolence*—she kept herself busy throughout the week. Afraid that her maids would notice that on the Sabbath she performed no work and guess that she was Jewish, she appointed a different maid for each day of the week. Those who ministered her during the week didn't see her rest on the Sabbath; the Sabbath maid, meanwhile, assumed that just as she did no work on the Sabbath, she did no work on *any* days of the week" (from *Yaaros Devash,* a homiletic work written by Rabbi Yonassan Eybeschuetz [1690–1796], a renowned Polish Torah scholar, and quoted in *The Megillah/The Book of Esther,* p. 57).

42. Quoted in Paton, *The Book of Esther,* p. 173.

43. In "Images of Women in the Talmud" Hauptman writes of the Talmudic view concerning a married woman's proper role:

> A woman's prime function in life is to concern herself with man's welfare and to provide for his physical comfort. A statement reported in the name of Elijah the prophet, and therefore most authoritative, explains how a woman serves as man's helpmeet: she converts grain into food and flax into clothing, thereby bringing light to his eyes and standing him on his feet. Or put succinctly by Rabbi Yossi: "I have never called my wife 'my wife,' only 'my home [house].' "

44. Or impaled on sticks; the Hebrew text simply states that they were "hung on a tree" or "hung on wood."

45. This does not refer to the biblical book of Chronicles, but rather to the Royal Annals routinely inscribed at the Persian court. According to the rabbis, the aborted assassination account was miraculously recorded (i.e., inscribed by itself, without human hands). That is why at a later time, when the sleepless king asked that the Royal Annals be read to him, the account of Mordecai's deed "was found written" (passive voice); in other words, the king remembered neither the incident, nor the recording of it (*Me'am Loez,* quoted in *The Megillah/The Book of Esther,* p. 64.)

46. According to Rashi, Haman claimed to have divine powers (see *The Megillah/The Book of Esther,* p. 64). Esther Rabbah VII 5, p. 82 preserves the view that Haman placed an embroidered image upon the breast of his garment, so that persons bowing before him were, at the same time, prostrating themselves before an image—an abhorrence to Jews.

47. For what follows, see Scherman, "An Overview," in *The Megillah/The Book of Esther,* pp. xxvii–xxix; Moore, *Esther,* p. 42; and Clines, *The Esther Scroll,* pp. 13–15 and passim.

48. See Berg's thorough analysis of the Mordecai genealogy and its significance in *The Book of Esther,* pp. 63–70.

49. In Deut. 25:17–19, part of Moses' purported final address to the Israelites, we read: "Remember what Amalek did to you on your journey, after you left Egypt—how, undeterred by fear of God, he surprised you on the march, when you were famished and weary, and cut down all the stragglers in your rear. Therefore, when the Lord your God grants you safety from all your enemies around you, in the land that the Lord your God is giving you as a hereditary portion, you shall blot out the memory of Amalek from under heaven. Do not forget!" See also Exod. 17, with its concluding verse: "And Moses built an altar and named it *Adonai-nissi* (i.e., "The Lord is my banner"). He said, 'It means, "Hand upon the throne of the Lord!" The Lord will be at war with Amalek throughout the ages.' "

50. *Megillah 13a,* p. 74.

51. "Pogrom" (meaning "like thunder") refers to an organized, often officially sanctioned, massacre of a minority group of people.

52. According to the text, the *pur* "was cast before Haman," suggesting that Haman procured the services of a professional astrologer or the like, rather than casting the lot himself.

53. Most likely, the lucky month and day were selected at one session, so that Haman need not return each day for eleven months until an appropriate one was identified (Moore, *Esther,* p. 38). According to the Septuagint, it was the thirteenth day of Adar; see Esth. 3:13.

54. The king politely refuses Haman's bribe, although he may have expected the silver to find its way into his coffers nonetheless.

55. These opinions are cited in *The Megillah/The Book of Esther,* p. 72.

56. From the commentary *Pirchai L'vanon,* cited in ibid., p. 43.

57. Moore (*Esther,* p. 47) suggests that sackcloth rendered the person wearing it ceremonially unclean.

58. The Hebrew verb used to describe Esther's reaction to Mordecai means, literally, to writhe. It is used in the Hebrew Bible to describe the behavior of women suffering the pains of childbirth (see, for example Isa. 51:2 [Sarah] and Deut. 32:18 [Yahweh laboring to bring forth Israel]). Some rabbis said that Esther was pregnant at the time. Learning of Haman's edict, she miscarried, never to conceive again. Others, however, believed that Esther later became pregnant for a second time and gave birth to Darius, the Persian king who granted the Jews permission to continue rebuilding their temple in Jerusalem (Ezra 6:1–12).

59. *The Megillah/The Book of Esther,* p. 82.

60. This opinion, attributed to Rabbi Meir Leibush (also referred to as Malbim, 1809–1879), is cited in *The Megillah/The Book of Esther),* pp. 78–79.

61. From *M'nos Halevi,* a commentary by Rabbi Shlomo Halevi Alkabetz (1505–1576), quoted in *The Megillah/The Book of Esther,* p. 87.

62. From *Ma'amar Mordechai,* a mid-sixteenth century commentary by Rabbi Shem Tov, cited in *The Megillah/The Book of Esther,* p. 90.

63. *Midrash Abba Gorion,* cited in *The Megillah/The Book of Esther,* p. 90.

64. Reliefs from Persepolis show Persian horses wearing crowns; see Moore, *Esther,* p. 65.

65. *Megillah 16a,* p. 95.

66. Clines, *The Esther Scroll,* p. 14.

67. *The Megillah/The Book of Esther,* p. 99. In *Esther,* Moore explains that "Zeresh is expressing here the views of the author, not her own. He knew better than any pagan woman the relevant biblical passages concerning the ultimate victory of the Jews over the Amalekites" (p. 66).

68. "If Mordecai, before whom *you have begun to fall,* is of Jewish stock, you will not overcome him; *you will fall* before him to your ruin."

69. *Megillah 16a,* p. 96.

70. As Moore (*Esther,* pp. 73–74) notes, "By identifying Ha-

man she had unmasked the villain, but she had also unmasked herself" [as a Jew].

71. This opinion, attributed to Vilna Gaon (Rabbi Eliyahu ben Shlomo Zalman of Vilna), appears in *The Megillah/The Book of Esther*, p. 103.

72. Haman's covered head following the mortifying escort episode (6:12) likely portended the covering of his head at this, his demise.

73. According to *Midrash Panim Acherim*, "Charbonah [=Harbonah] said: This is not the only crime committed by Haman, for he was an accomplice of the conspirators, Bigsan (Bigthan) and Teresh. His enmity against Mordechai dates back to the time when he bared that assassination attempt. Haman erected the gallows to avenge himself against Mordechai for his loyalty to the King." Quoted in *The Megillah/The Book of Esther*, p. 105.

74. Darr, "Esther and Additions to Esther," p. 175.

75. Obviously, Esther is using her most persuasive rhetoric!

76. See Clines, *The Esther Scroll*, pp. 17–21.

77. According to the rabbis, Esther hated her royal robes and only wore them on her first uninvited visit to the throne room because she knew they made her more beautiful and difficult to refuse (*M'nos Halevi*, cited in *The Megillah/The Book of Esther*), p. 83.

78. So the sixteenth-century commentator, Rabbi Elisha Galico, cited in ibid., p. 115.

79. According to *D'na Pashra*, a commentary written by Rabbi Eliyahu Shlomo Avraham haKohen (d. 1729), the joy of Susa was so complete even its stones shouted in celebration. Quoted in *The Megillah/The Book of Esther*, p. 115.

80. What does "the fear of the Jews" mean? Some modern commentators argue that it connotes "dread of the Jews"; others believe the phrase refers to awe and reverence for them. In this context, however, both meanings may have been intended by the author.

81. See the thorough analysis by Clines in *The Esther Scroll*, especially pp. 94–114 and 151–158.

82. See Anderson, "The Book of Esther," p. 867.

83. See below. Most modern scholars do not believe that Purim was originally a Jewish festival. Rather, the diaspora Jews adopted a pagan festival and then explained its "origin" with

the story of Esther and Mordecai's deliverance of Persian Jewry. They do not agree, however, about the identity of the underlying festival itself. Some scholars have attempted to link it with a Babylonian myth (in which case, the names "Esther" and "Mordecai" may derive from Ishtar and Marduk, two Babylonian deities). Others, however, point to a Persian festival—either a festival for the dead or a new year celebration.

84. *Nachal Eshkol*, a homiletical work composed by Rabbi Chaim Yosef David Azulai (1724–1806), quoted in *The Megillah/The Book of Esther*, p. 121. Other rabbis (Rashi, Ibn Ezra) claimed that by refusing to take their enemies' possessions, the Jews cleared themselves of any suspicion that they were acting out of greed, rather than self-defense. See ibid., pp. 120–121.

85. *M'nos Halevi*, quoted in *The Megillah/The Book of Esther*, p. 122.

86. Paton, *Esther*, p. 288.

87. Lev. 27:34 has been cited as the biblical basis for the view that only Mosaic laws and festivals should be observed by Jews. See Moore, *Esther*, p. XXXI.

88. Hence, when we read in 6:1 that "sleep deserted the king," the rabbis explain that not only was Ahasuerus unable to sleep, but also the heavenly King's repose was disturbed by the Jews' cries (*The Megillah/The Book of Esther*, p. 90–91).

89. The Talmud (*Chullin 139b*), quoted in Scherman, "An Overview," p. xv, asserts that there is a reference to Esther in the Torah, in Deut. 31:18: "And I will hide my face." One need not know Hebrew to recognize the similarity between *'ster* ("Esther") and *'astir* ("I will hide"). By finding a "reference" to Esther in the Torah, the rabbis sought to enhance the book's authority.

90. The Septuagint is the Greek translation of the Old Testament and the Apocrypha. It was produced in Alexandria during the final three centuries B.C.E. For Greek-speaking Jews (including Paul the Apostle), the Septuagint was the Bible.

91. Addition B, for example, purports to be the content of the first edict, issued by Ahasuerus at Haman's request. The text of the second edict appears in Addition E. They were undoubtedly added to satisfy curiosity and to bolster the book's claims to historical credibility.

92. Some women value Vashti's rebellion but recognize and prize a rebellious streak in Esther as well. In *Just a Sister Away*,

for example, Renita Weems suggests that Ahasuerus must have been attracted to independent women, since he rid himself of one only to choose another. "His first wife, Queen Vashti, refused to come to the king when summoned," she writes. "His second wife, Queen Esther, went to the king without summons. The similarity of the two women's defiance is striking" (p. 99). Vashti receives considerable praise from Weems, whose primary focus is the enormous sacrifices and contributions of women who marry public leaders. Nevertheless, Weems clearly regards Esther as a fitting heir to Vashti's legacy of courage.

93. Laffey, *An Introduction to the Old Testament*, pp. 214–215.

94. Ibid., p. 215. As we have seen, the rabbis' treatment of Vashti suggests that they, too, were intolerant of a disobedient wife, even if her husband was a wicked pagan king.

95. *Braided Streams: Esther and a Woman's Way of Growing* (San Diego: LuraMedia, 1985), p. 40.

96. Ibid., p. 42.

97. Laffey, *An Introduction to the Old Testament*, p. 216.

98. White, "Esther: A Feminine Model," pp. 161–177.

99. Here, White stands squarely within the rabbinical interpretive tradition.

100. Ibid., p. 169.

101. Ibid., p. 170.

102. In *Braided Streams*, Bankson invites readers to reflect upon and share their own stories in the midst of reading about Esther. She finds in Esther's story a female counterpart to the story of Moses:

> Symbolically, Esther moved inward to meet God, while Moses fled to a far land. Esther entered the king's harem, left behind her mentor and religious community, then even her bodily safety, until she was stripped of all her male protectors. She came face-to-face with God in her own "dark night of the soul." After that three-day period "in the tomb," she began to move outward from the centeredness in her own body, out into the world of public affairs" (p. 15).

Bankson's emphasis upon spiritual dimensions of the book benefits from her decision to use the expanded Septuagint version of Esther (from *The Jerusalem Bible*).

103. Esther: A Feminine Model," p. 173.

104. Laffey, *An Introduction to the Old Testament*, p. 216.

Selected Bibliography

Ackroyd, Peter. *Exile and Restoration: A Study of Hebrew Thought of the Sixth Century* B.C. Old Testament Library. Philadelphia: Westminster Press, 1968.

Adler, Elaine June. "The Background for the Metaphor of Covenant as Marriage in the Hebrew Bible." Ph.D. diss., University of California, 1989.

Alter, Robert. "Introduction to the Old Testament." In *The Literary Guide to the Bible.* Ed. Robert Alter and Frank Kermode. Cambridge, Mass.: Harvard University Press, 1987.

Anderson, Bernhard W. "The Book of Esther: Introduction and Exegesis." In *The Interpreter's Bible.* Vol. 3, pp. 823–874. New York: Abingdon Press, 1954.

―――. *Understanding the Old Testament.* 4th ed. Englewood Cliffs, N.J.: Prentice-Hall, 1986.

Bankson, Marjory Zoet. *Braided Streams: Esther and a Woman's Way of Growing.* San Diego: LuraMedia, 1985.

Bardtke, Hans. *Das Buch Esther.* Kommentar zum Alten Testament. Gütersloh: Mohn, 1963.

Barr, James. *Holy Scripture: Canon, Authority, Criticism.* Philadelphia: Westminster Press, 1983.

Bass, Dorothy C. " 'In Christian Firmness and Christian Meekness': Feminism and Pacificism in Antebellum America." In *Immaculate and Powerful: The Female in Sacred Image and Social Reality,* pp. 201–225. Ed. Clarissa C. Atkinson, Constance H. Buchanan, and Margaret R. Miles. Boston: Beacon Press, 1985.

―――. "Women's Studies and Biblical Studies: An Historical Perspective." *Journal for the Study of the Old Testament* 22 (1982): 6–12.

Beattie, D. R. G. *Jewish Exegesis of the Book of Ruth.* Journal for the Study of the Old Testament Supplement Series, no. 2. Sheffield: JSOT, 1977.

Berg, Sandra Beth. *The Book of Esther: Motifs, Themes, and Structure.* Society of Biblical Literature Dissertation Series, no. 44. Missoula, Mont.: Scholars Press, 1979.

Bettenhausen, Elizabeth. "Hagar Revisited: Surrogacy, Alienation, and Motherhood." *Christianity and Crisis* 47 (1987): 157–159.

Bird, Phyllis. "Images of Women in the Old Testament." In *Religion and Sexism: Images of Woman in the Jewish and Christian Traditions.* Ed. Rosemary Radford Ruether. New York: Simon & Schuster, 1974.

————. " 'To Play the Harlot:' An Inquiry into an Old Testament Metaphor." In *Gender and Difference in Ancient Israel*, pp. 75–94. Ed. Peggy L. Day. Minneapolis: Fortress Press, 1989.

Bledstein, Adrien J. "The Trials of Sarah." *Judaism* 30 (1981): 411–417.

Boldrey, Richard and Joyce. *Chauvinist or Feminist? Paul's View of Women.* Grand Rapids: Baker Book House, 1976.

Booij, Thijs. "Hagar's Words in Genesis 16:13b." *Vetus Testamentum* 30 (1980): 1–7.

Booth, Wayne C. *The Rhetoric of Fiction.* Chicago: University of Chicago Press, 1961.

Brock, Sebastian P. "Genesis 22: Where was Sarah?" *Expository Times* 96 (1984): 14–17.

Bronner, L. L. "Gynomorphic Imagery in Exilic Isaiah (40–66)." *Dor le Dor* 12 (1983–84): 71–83.

Brueggemann, Walter. *Genesis.* Interpretation. Atlanta: John Knox Press, 1982.

————. " 'Impossibility' and Epistemology in the Faith Tradition of Abraham and Sarah (Gen. 18:1–15)." *Zeitschrift für die alttestamentliche Wissenschaft* 94 (1982): 615–634.

————. "Will Our Faith Have Children?" *Word and World: Theology for Christian Ministry* 3 (1983): 272–283.

Calloway, Mary. *Sing, O Barren One: A Study in Comparative Midrash.* Society of Biblical Literature Dissertation Series, no. 91. Atlanta: Scholars Press, 1986.

Camp, Claudia V. "Female Voice, Written Word: Women and Authority in Hebrew Scripture." In *Embodied Love: Sensuality and Relationship as Feminist Values,* pp. 97–113. Ed. Paula M. Cooey, Sharon A. Farmer, and Mary Ellen Ross. New York: Harper & Row, 1987.

Campbell, Edward F., Jr. *Ruth.* Anchor Bible. Garden City, N.Y.: Doubleday, 1975.

Cannon, Katie Geneva. "The Emergence of Black Feminist Consciousness." In *Feminist Interpretation of the Bible,* pp. 30–40. Ed. Letty M. Russell. Philadelphia: Westminster Press, 1985.

Childs, Brevard S. *The Book of Exodus: A Critical, Theological Commentary.* Old Testament Library. Philadelphia: Westminster Press, 1974.

―――. *Introduction to the Old Testament as Scripture.* Philadelphia: Fortress Press, 1979.

Clines, David J. A. *The Esther Scroll: The Story of the Story.* Journal for the Study of the Old Testament Supplement Series, no. 30. Sheffield: JSOT Press, 1984.

Corre, Alan. *Understanding the Talmud.* New York: KTAV Publishing House, 1975.

Cross, Frank Moore. *Canaanite Myth and Hebrew Epic. Essays in the History of the Religion of Israel.* Cambridge, Mass.: Harvard University Press, 1973.

Darr, John A. " 'Glorified in the Presence of Kings': A Literary-Critical Study of Herod the Tetrarch in Luke-Acts." Ph.D. diss., Vanderbilt University, 1987.

Darr, Katheryn Pfisterer. "Esther and Additions to Esther." In *The Books of the Bible.* Ed. Bernhard W. Anderson. Vol. 1, *The Old Testament/The Hebrew Bible,* pp. 173–179. New York: Charles Scribner's Sons, 1989.

―――. "Like Warrior, Like Woman: Destruction and Deliverance in Isaiah 42:10–17." *Catholic Biblical Quarterly* 49 (1987): 560–571.

Denton, Robert C., ed. *The Oxford Annotated Bible.* New York: Oxford University Press. 1962.

Dever, William G. "Syro-Palestinian and Biblical Archaeology." In *The Hebrew Bible and Its Modern Interpreters,* pp. 31–74. Ed. Douglas A. Knight and Gene M. Tucker. Philadelphia/Chico: Fortress/Scholars, 1985.

Encyclopaedia Judaica, 1971 ed. S.v. "Abraham," by David Kadosh.

―――. S.v. "Aggadah."

————. S.v. "Midrash," by David Herr.

Epstein, Isidore, ed. *Baba Bathra*. Tr. Maurice Simon. In *The Babylonian Talmud*. London: Soncino, 1935.

————. *Megillah*. Tr. Maurice Simon. In *The Babylonian Talmud*. New York: Soncino, 1938.

————. *Sanhedrin*. Tr. H. Freedman. In *The Babylonian Talmud*. New York: Soncino, 1935.

Exum, J. Cheryl. " 'Mother in Israel': A Familiar Figure Reconsidered." In *Feminist Interpretation of the Bible*, pp. 73–85. Ed. Letty M. Russell. Philadelphia: Westminster Press, 1985.

Fiorenza, Elisabeth Schüssler. *In Memory of Her: A Feminist Theological Reconstruction of Christian Origins*. New York: Crossroad/Continuum, 1983.

————. "Remembering the Past in Creating the Future: Historical-Critical Scholarship and Feminist Biblical Interpretation." In *Feminist Perspectives on Biblical Scholarship*, pp. 43–63. Ed. Adela Yarbro Collins. Society of Biblical Literature Centennial Biblical Scholarship in North America, no. 10. Decatur, Ga.: Scholars Press, 1985.

Fishbane, Michael. "Jewish Biblical Exegesis: Presuppositions and Principles." In *Scripture in the Jewish and Christian Traditions: Authority, Interpretation, Relevance*, pp. 91–110. Ed. Frederick E. Greenspahn. Nashville: Abingdon Press, 1982.

Freedman, H. "The Book of Genesis." In *The Soncino Chumash*. Ed. A. Cohen. Hindhead, England: Soncino, 1947.

Freedman, H. and Maurice Simon, eds. *Midrash Rabbah*. Vol. 1, *Genesis*. 3rd ed. Tr. H. Freedman. London: Soncino, 1983.

————. *Midrash Rabbah*. Vol. 3, *Exodus*. Tr. S. M. Lehrman. London: Soncino, 1983.

————. *Midrash Rabbah*. Vol. 8, *Ruth*. 3rd ed. Tr. L. Rabinowitz. London: Soncino, 1983.

————. *Midrash Rabbah*. Vol. 9, *Esther*. 3rd ed. Tr. Maurice Simon. London: Soncino, 1983.

Fuchs, Esther. "A Jewish Feminist Reading of the Hagar Stories." Unpublished paper.

————. "The Literary Characterization of Mothers and Sexual Politics in the Hebrew Bible." In *Feminist Perspectives on Biblical Scholarship*. Ed. Adela Yarbro Collins. Society of Biblical Literature Centennial Biblical Scholarship in North America, no. 10. Decatur, Ga.: Scholars Press, 1985.

Gifford, Carolyn de Swarte. "American Women and the Bible:

The Nature of Woman as a Hermeneutical Issue." In *Feminist Perspectives on Biblical Scholarship*, pp. 11–33. Ed. Adela Yarbro Collins. Society of Biblical Literature Centennial Biblical Scholarship in North America, no. 10. Decatur, Ga.: Scholars Press, 1985.

Ginzberg, Louis. *The Legends of the Jews*. Vol. 1. Tr. Henrietta Szold. Philadelphia: The Jewish Publication Society of America, 1909.

Gordis, Robert. *Megillat Esther: The Masoretic Hebrew Text with Introduction, New Translation, and Commentary*. New York: The Rabbinical Assembly, 1972.

Gordon, Cynthia. "Hagar: A Throw-Away Character Among the Matriarchs?" *The Society of Biblical Literature Seminar Papers* 24 (1985): 271–277.

Gottwald, Norman K. *The Hebrew Bible: A Socio-Literary Introduction*. Philadelphia: Fortress Press, 1985.

Green, Barbara. "The Plot of the Biblical Story of Ruth." *Journal for the Study of the Old Testament* 23 (1982): 55–68.

Gruber, Mayer. "The Motherhood of God in Second Isaiah." *Revue Biblique* 90 (1983): 351–359.

Hackett, Jo Ann. "Can A Sexist Model Liberate Us?: Ancient Near Eastern 'Fertility' Goddesses." *Journal of Feminist Studies in Religion* 5 (1989): 65–76.

———. "Rehabilitating Hagar: Fragments of an Epic Pattern." In *Gender and Difference in Ancient Israel*, pp. 12–27. Ed. Peggy L. Day. Philadelphia: Fortress Press, 1989.

Hauptman, Judith. "Images of Woman in the Talmud." In *Religion and Sexism: Images of Woman in the Jewish and Christian Traditions*. Ed. Rosemary Radford Ruether. New York: Simon & Schuster, 1974.

Humphreys, W. Lee. "The Story of Esther and Mordecai: An Early Jewish Novella." In *Saga, Legend, Tale, Novella, Fable: Narrative Forms in Old Testament Literature*. pp. 97–113. Ed. George W. Coats. Sheffield: JSOT, 1985.

The Interpreter's Dictionary of the Bible, 1962. S.v. "Abraham," by L. Hicks.

———. S.v. "Arnon," by E. D. Grohman.

———. S.v. "Josephus, Flavius," by J. Goldin.

———. S.v. "Marriage," by C. R. Taber.

———. S.v. "Moab," by E. D. Grohman.

———. S.v. "Slavery in the OT," by I. Mendelsohn.

The Interpreter's Dictionary of the Bible, Supplementary Volume, 1976. S.v. "God, Nature of, in the Old Testament," by Phyllis Trible.

Krentz, Edgar. *The Historical-Critical Method.* Ed. Gene M. Tucker. Guides to Biblical Scholarship: Old Testament Series. Philadelphia: Fortress Press, 1975.

Laffey, Alice L. *An Introduction to the Old Testament: A Feminist Perspective.* Philadelphia: Fortress Press, 1988.

Leith, Mary Joan Winn. "Verse and Reverse: The Transformation of the Woman, Israel, in Hosea 1–3." In *Gender and Difference in Ancient Israel.* Ed. Peggy L. Day. Philadelphia: Fortress Press, 1989.

Luther, Martin. *Luther's Works.* Ed. Helmut T. Lehmann. Vol. 54, *Table Talk.* Ed. and tr. Theodore G. Tappert. Philadelphia: Fortress Press, 1967.

McEvenue, Sean E. "A Comparison of Narrative Styles in the Hagar Stories." *Semeia* 3 (1975): 64–80.

McFague, Sallie. *Metaphorical Theology: Models of God in Religious Language.* Philadelphia: Fortress Press, 1982.

Meyers, Carol. *Discovering Eve: Ancient Israelite Women in Context.* New York: Oxford University Press, 1988.

Millet, Kate. *Sexual Politics.* New York: Ballatine, 1969.

Moore, Carey. *Esther.* Anchor Bible. Garden City, N.J.: Doubleday, 1971.

Neusner, Jacob. "Scripture and Mishnah: Authority and Selectivity." In *Scripture in the Jewish and Christian Traditions: Authority, Interpretation, Relevance*, pp. 65–85. Ed. Frederick E. Greenspahn. Nashville: Abingdon Press, 1982.

———. *What is Midrash?* Guides to Biblical Scholarship: New Testament Series. Ed. Dan O. Via. Philadelphia: Fortress Press, 1987.

Nunnally-Cox, Janice. *Foremothers: Women of the Bible.* New York: Seabury Press, 1981.

Oden, Robert. *The Bible Without Theology.* San Francisco: Harper & Row, 1987.

Osiek, Carolyn. "The Feminist and the Bible: Hermeneutical Alternatives." In *Feminist Perspectives on Biblical Scholarship.* Ed. Adela Yarbro Collins. Society of Biblical Literature Centennial Biblical Scholarship in North America, no. 10. Decatur, Ga.: Scholars Press, 1985.

Overholt, Thomas W. *Channels of Prophecy: The Social Dynamics of Prophetic Activity.* Philadelphia: Fortress Press, 1989.

Parker, Simon B. *The Pre-Biblical Narrative Tradition.* SBL Resources for Biblical Study, no. 24. Atlanta: Scholars Press, 1989.

Paton, Lewis Bayles. *The Book of Esther.* The International Critical Commentary. New York: Charles Scribner's Sons, 1908.

Plaut, W. Gunther. *The Book of Proverbs.* New York: Union of American Hebrew Congregations, 1961.

Polzin, Robert M. "The Ancestress of Israel in Danger." *Semeia* 3 (1975): 81–98.

Pritchard, James L., ed. *Ancient Near Eastern Texts.* 3rd ed. with supplement. Princeton: Princeton University Press, 1969.

Rad, Gerhard von. *Genesis.* Old Testament Library. Tr. John H. Marks. Philadelphia: Westminster Press, 1961.

Rashi (Rabbi Shelomoh Yitschaki, Solomon ben Isaac). *Commentaries on the Pentateuch.* Tr. Chaim Pearl. New York: W. W. Norton & Co., 1970.

Rauber, D. F. "Literary Values in the Bible: The Book of Ruth." *Journal of Biblical Literature* 89 (1970): 27–37.

Rich, Adrienne. *Of Woman Born: Motherhood as Experience and Institution.* New York: W. W. Norton & Co., 1976.

Ruether, Rosemary Radford. "Feminist Interpretation: A Method of Correlation." In *Feminist Interpretation of the Bible.* Ed. Letty M. Russell, Philadelphia: Westminster Press, 1985.

———. *New Woman-New Earth: Sexist Ideologies and Human Liberation.* New York: Crossroad, 1975.

Sarna, Nahum M. "Genesis 23: The Cave of Machpelah." *Hebrew Studies* 23 (1982): 17–21.

Scherman, Nosson. *Zemiroth: Sabbath Songs with Additional Sephardic Zemiroth.* Brooklyn: Mesorah Publications, 1979.

——— and Meir Zlotowitz, eds. *The Book of Ruth/Megillas Ruth: A New Translation with a Commentary Anthologized from Talmudic, Midrashic and Rabbinic Sources.* ArtScroll Tanach Series. Brooklyn: Mesorah Publications, 1976.

Schmitt, J. J. "The Motherhood of God." *Revue Biblique* 92 (1985): 557–569.

Setel, T. Drorah. "Feminist Insights and the Question of Method." In *Feminist Perspectives on Biblical Scholarship.* Ed. Adela Yarbro Collins. Society of Biblical Literature Centen-

nial Biblical Scholarship in North America, no. 10. Decatur,
Ga.: Scholars Press, 1985.
————. "Prophets and Pornography: Female Sexual Imagery
in Hosea." In *Feminist Interpretation of the Bible*. Ed. Letty M.
Russell. Philadelphia: Westminster Press, 1985.
Silberman, Lou H. "*Aggadah* and *Halakhah:* Ethos and Ethics
in Rabbinic Judaism." In *The Life of Covenant: The Challenge
of Contemporary Judaism (Essays in Honor of Herman E. Schaal-
man)*. Ed. Joseph A. Edelheit. Chicago: Spertus College of
Judaica Press, 1986.
Speiser, E. A. *Genesis*. Anchor Bible, Garden City, N.J.: Dou-
bleday, 1964.
Spinoza, Benedict de. *The Chief Works of Benedict de Spinoza*. Tr.
with an introduction by R. H. M. Elwes. Vol. 1, *Introduction,
Tractatus Theologico-Politicus, Tractatus Politicus*. 2nd ed., re-
vised. London: George Bell & Sons, 1889.
Stagg, Evelyn and Frank. *Woman in the World of Jesus*. Philadel-
phia: Westminster Press, 1978.
Talmon, S. "Wisdom in the Book of Esther." *Vetus Testamentum*
13 (1963): 419–455.
Tamez, Elsa. "The Woman Who Complicated the History of
Salvation." Tr. Betsy Yeager. In *New Eyes for Reading*. Eds.
John S. Pobee and Bärbel von Wartenberg-Potter. Oak Park,
Ill.: Meyer-Stone Books, 1986.
Tanakh. Philadelphia: The Jewish Publication Society, 5746/
1985.
Teubal, Savina. *Sarah the Priestess: The First Matriarch of Genesis*.
Athens, Ohio: Ohio University Press, 1984.
Thistlethwaite, Susan Brooks. "Every Two Minutes: Battered
Women and Feminist Interpretation." In *Feminist Interpreta-
tion of the Bible*. Ed. Letty M. Russell. Philadelphia: Westmin-
ster Press, 1985.
Tolbert, Mary Ann. "Defining the Problem: The Bible and
Feminist Hermeneutics." *Semeia* 28 (1983): 113–126.
Trible, Phyllis. *God and the Rhetoric of Sexuality*. Overtures to
Biblical Theology, no. 2. Philadelphia: Fortress Press, 1978.
————. *Texts of Terror: Literary-Feminist Readings of Biblical Nar-
ratives*. Overtures to Biblical Theology, no. 13. Philadelphia:
Fortress Press, 1984.
Twersky, Isadore. *Introduction to the Code of Maimonides (Mishneh*

Torah). Yale Judaica Series, no. 22. New Haven, Conn.: Yale University Press, 1980.

Umansaky, Ellen M. "Beyond Androcentrism: Feminist Challenges to Judaism," *Journal of Reform Judaism* 37 (1990): 25–35.

Walker, Alice. *In Search of Our Mothers' Gardens: Womanist Prose.* San Diego: Harcourt Brace Jovanovich, 1983.

Weems, Renita. *Just A Sister Away: A Womanist Vision of Women's Relationships in the Bible.* San Diego: LuraMedia, 1988.

Wellhausen, Julius. *Prolegomena to the History of Ancient Israel.* 1878. Reprint. Gloucester, Mass.: Peter Smith, 1973.

Westermann, Claus. *Genesis.* Tr. David E. Green. Grand Rapids: Wm. B. Eerdmans Publishing Co., 1987.

White, Sidnie Ann. "Esther: A Feminine Model for Jewish Diaspora." In *Gender and Difference in Ancient Israel.* Ed. Peggy L. Day. Philadelphia: Fortress Press, 1989.

Wiesel, Elie. "In the Bible: Ruth or Welcoming Stranger." Presented as the first Andrew W. Mellon Lecture in the Humanities, Boston University, March 12, 1990.

———. "Ishmael and Hagar." In *The Life of Covenant: The Challenge of Contemporary Judaism (Essays in Honor of Herman E. Schaalman).* Ed. Joseph A. Edelheit. Chicago: Spertus College of Judaica Press, 1986.

Wilson, Robert R. *Prophecy and Society in Ancient Israel.* Philadelphia: Fortress Press, 1980.

———. *Sociological Approaches to the Old Testament.* Guides to Biblical Scholarship: Old Testament Series. Philadelphia: Fortress Press, 1984.

Zlotowitz, Meir, tr. and ed. *The Megillah/The Book of Esther: A New Translation with a Commentary Anthologized from Talmudic, Midrashic and Rabbinic Sources.* 2nd ed., rev. and corrected. ArtScroll Tanach Series. Brooklyn: Mesorah Publications, 1981.

Index